Slacking

A Guide to Ivy League
Miseducation

Slacking

A Guide to Ivy League Miseducation

ADAM KISSEL

RACHEL ALEXANDER CAMBRE

MADISON MARINO DOAN

New York · London

Encounter
BOOKS

First American edition published in 2025 by Encounter Books, an activity of Encounter for Culture and Education, Inc., a nonprofit, tax exempt corporation.
Encounter Books website address: www.encounterbooks.com

Manufactured in Canada and printed on
acid-free paper. The paper used in this publication meets
the minimum requirements of ANSI/NISO Z39.48–1992 (R 1997)
(*Permanence of Paper*).

FIRST AMERICAN EDITION

LIBRARY OF CONGRESS CATALOGING-IN-PUBLICATION DATA IS
AVAILABLE

Information for this title can be found at the Library of
Congress website under the following
ISBN 978-1-64177-459-8 and LCCN 2025003863.

CONTENTS

INTRODUCTION | *page* 1

CORNELL UNIVERSITY | *page* 5

YALE UNIVERSITY | *page* 31

UNIVERSITY OF PENNSYLVANIA | *page* 47

HARVARD UNIVERSITY | *page* 69

PRINCETON UNIVERSITY | *page* 89

DARTMOUTH COLLEGE | *page* 111

COLUMBIA UNIVERSITY | *page* 135

BROWN UNIVERSITY | *page* 147

CONCLUSION: SLACKERS OR STRIVERS? | *page* 155

INDEX | *page* 157

INTRODUCTION

Don't trust the Ivy League to produce well-educated students.

The eight institutions that make up the Ivy League are among the most selective in the United States, and their graduates occupy the elite echelons of American life. Parents often spend $80,000 or more per year for their children to attend Princeton, Harvard, Yale, Penn, Columbia, Brown, Cornell, or Dartmouth and have an opportunity to punch a ticket to the top.

But what really happens there? Do graduates really join "the fellowship of educated men and women," as Harvard used to assert each year at its commencement ceremony?

Some do. Many don't.

Like most American colleges, most of the Ivies grant significant latitude in the undergraduate curriculum. (Columbia is the only exception.) Students not only choose a major—from as many as ninety options—but they also choose the content of their core curriculum. Core curricula historically guaranteed consistency for undergraduates, reflecting a wise faculty's determination of the knowledge and academic skills most worth having. Today, however, most general education requirements in the Ivies are so general—some arts here, some sciences there—that they are simply another opportunity for undirected self-actualization. Hundreds of course options can fulfill each "requirement."

These options, moreover, vary tremendously—from serious, rigorous, and open to challenge, to whimsical, activist, and tendentious. This variation is greatest in the humanities and social sciences. For every course seeking to develop a broader or deeper understanding of man, nature, and the cosmos, there are dozens preoccupied with pop culture, identity politics, progressive activism, or hyper-specialization.

Writing requirements are even worse. Putatively about writing, such courses indulge the moral and political conceits of their instructors. At the other extreme, most courses that meet science requirements actually teach science, even though light courses are available for slackers. (At Cornell, the course discussing Disney films to learn about animals is an exception, and Columbia still offers Physics for Poets.)

A generation ago, the critique of Ivy League curricula was that a student could graduate without being required to take any Shakespeare, American history, or Western civilization. That complaint remains well-grounded. Today, the situation is worse: Can a serious student find even *one* core course on Shakespeare or America worth taking?

By not providing a content-rich core curriculum—a set of required courses in the arts and sciences—but instead allowing students to choose from a wide range of courses to fulfill vague distribution requirements, most of the Ivies risk having students graduate with what the American Council of Trustees and Alumni calls a "thin and patchy education, with no guarantee that they have mastered a core set of facts or skills." Absent strong curricular requirements, universities cannot guarantee that students "learn what they need to know to be informed citizens, effective workers, and lifelong learners."

Fortunately, a strong education remains available to Ivy students in most areas of general education. They will have to work for it and get wise advice. But by far, Ivy League students are offered, and thus receive, a truly substandard education by any reasonable measure. Dante or Cardi B? Every educated man and woman ought to know the difference.

This book shows the best and the worst that Ivy League general education courses offer.

What This Book Is and Isn't

This book has eight chapters, one for each of the Ivies. Each chapter introduces the undergraduate requirements and then shows the highlights and lowlights of the courses available to meet each requirement. Each chapter ends with examples of a worst, weak, terrible course of study for slackers or activists and a best, strong, recommended course of study for serious students.

Do not expect consistency in presentation from one institution to the next; each institution is unique. We save the two extremes for the final two chapters: Unlike the others, Columbia includes several content-rich core requirements with common readings across all sections. Meanwhile, Brown's only common content requirement is two writing courses.

This book also does not examine the rest of the curriculum at each institution, leaving the requirements of majors (sometimes called "concentrations") and non-core electives for another time. Graduate programs, likewise, are left for later. Finally, when an institution has different requirements for different college students, we choose the arts-and-sciences bachelor's requirements over, for example, the requirements tailored for engineering students.

The chapters were written in the spring and summer of 2024. Course listings for academic year 2024–25 were not necessarily available for each requirement when the chapters were written. Furthermore, course listings are added and subtracted from week to week, and course names and descriptions also frequently change. Note well that the lists of discouraged or recommended courses may not be feasible in practice because not all courses are offered each term. What is presented here are illustrative snapshots of the general education curricula rather than definitive course recommendations, which would be a moving target for institutions that insist on using distribution requirements. Endnotes are omitted to avoid the need for hundreds of citations. Course names and descriptions are silently edited where they conflict with the book's style guide.

Readers also should understand that many course descriptions do not include the readings. Even less can one readily determine from afar how a particular course is taught. It was reported in September, for example, that one of the better-known protesters at Columbia is now teaching one of its Western Civilization courses. Moreover, some "best" and "worst" courses may be misclassified. But we do know that teaching Dante badly at least exposes a student to Dante, whereas it's hard to see how teaching Cardi B (as at Cornell) is edifying at all.

CORNELL UNIVERSITY

U ndergraduates in Cornell University's College of Arts and Sciences must complete "distribution requirements" and additional credits in order to graduate. The requirements include broad subject areas and proficiencies, including in writing and a foreign language. Cornell also requires two one-credit classes of physical education across the first year, plus a swim test (or swim classes), except for transfer and advanced placement students.

Overall, there are many ways to get a strong general education as an Arts and Sciences student. But there are also many ways to get a weak and useless education at Cornell. The exception is in the hard sciences, where almost everything to choose from is challenging and valuable.

Why Get a General Education at Cornell?

Cornell expects certain "learning outcomes" for all undergraduates and particular outcomes for Arts and Sciences students.

The eleven general outcomes are summarized here as eight overlapping proficiencies:

- Gain disciplinary knowledge, including systematic and technical understanding, and be able to synthesize ideas in the field.
- Apply analysis and critique to arguments and problems.
- Express one's ideas well, both orally and in writing.
- Reason scientifically and quantitatively, including problem definition and investigation.
- Direct one's own learning and behavior. Work productively.
- Assess and use information.
- Understand and engage across cultural perspectives. Engage in the community.
- Make good moral judgments, reason ethically, and "promote honesty, trust, fairness, respect, and responsibility."

The two areas that do the most work here are disciplinary knowledge (in one's major) and self-directed learning (for the rest). This is because Cornell does not truly check whether students are becoming proficient in these areas. Instead—taking Arts and Sciences as the primary example—a wide range of distribution requirements and electives fulfill Cornell's graduation requirements. Students can diverge wildly in the courses they take and the proficiencies, if any, they develop.

The College of Arts and Sciences (CAS) specifies what it offers and why it has chosen its curriculum. CAS introduces its curriculum as a "broad spectrum of study" that helps students "develop their ability to think in complex ways" about what they will face throughout their lives. This means "honing one's critical and imaginative capacities, learning about oneself in nature and culture, and gaining experience with views of the world radically unlike one's own." But the way to these outcomes "is highly individual" and designed by "each student and his/her faculty advisor."

In particular, CAS expects the following five "educational outcomes." Note that Cornell has chosen a "ways of knowing" approach, which is how many colleges justify having distribution requirements rather than any body of knowledge that an educated person ought to know. Quoting directly, these are:

- Familiarity with the several different ways of knowing that are reflected in the various disciplines and fields of study within the humanities, social sciences, mathematics, and sciences.
- Cultural breadth (both geographical and temporal).
- Effective writing and quantitative skills.
- Facility in a foreign language beyond the introductory level.
- Imaginative and critical thinking. ("Students are expected to concentrate on one particular field through which they develop their imaginative and critical thinking capacities. They must demonstrate a thorough grasp of their selected field.")

Since the fifth outcome is expected to develop through a student's major, it is the first four outcomes, plus the university-wide outcomes, that are to be developed by means of the distribution requirements and electives.

Writing

In writing, Cornell requires two courses across two semesters. Cornell boasts more than 100 options across more than thirty subject areas. The idea is to place writing skills within a discipline relevant to the student's other academic work. Expository and academic writing, however, are not the only kinds of writing that students produce.

According to the "Fall 2023 First-Year Writing Seminars" brochure, a Humanities Core Course can meet the requirement. So can courses called "Short Stories," "Greek Myth," "Robots," "The Craft of Storytelling: Race, Gender, and Postcolonial Writing," "Educational Inequality and Reform Efforts in the US," "Race and Colonialism in Modern Germany," "The Search for the Historical Muhammad," "Philosophical Conversations: Ethics and Moral Psychology in Technology," "Grievance: In Three Texts," and "Queer Girlhood in American Pop Culture."

Slackers who take "Queer Girlhood" are provided the course's truth that "*Archie* [c]omics, Barbies, model horses, and girls' organizations like the Camp Fire Girls were used to teach girls how to perform certain idealized forms of girlhood which centered heterosexuality, femininity, and whiteness." The writing assignments include "fanfiction [sic]." The course also includes such important texts as the film *Mean Girls*, the television show *Powerpuff Girls*, and Western classics *Twilight* and *The Hunger Games*. Without these, how can an American claim cultural literacy?

The three "texts" of the "Grievance" course are *The Crucible*, the Declaration of Independence, and "the event of January 6th, 2021," which all exemplify, students are told, "the on-going history of grievance in American politics." The course declares that the January 6th "text" is not an "aberration" but an example of America's "constituent norm" of political grievance.

Inscrutably, "Embodied Deep Ecological Living" is an Asian Studies course that meets the requirement. It's "for students who have genuine interests in practicing deep ecological living." Writing assignments can include "curatorial statement, manifesto of deep ecology, etc."

Insensibly, a writing course from Ecology and Evolutionary Biology takes as truth that the "widespread genocide of Native Americans left [North American] ecosystems untended until European descendants began to alter land use management." The course "will give students the opportunity to go beyond the land acknowledgement."

Inevitably, "Power and Politics: Liberalism and Marxism" treats "the Marxist critique of liberalism" with readings from Karl Marx and Benjamin Constant, among others. Students ask, "Is liberal pluralism an adequate response to the intersections of race, gender, and class oppression?" Similarly, the course "Liberalism and Neoliberalism" examines "the role that liberalism plays in the current neoliberal political order," whatever that is, using Marx, Rawls, Du Bois, and Angela Davis.

The English Department (ahem, "Department of Literatures in English") offers "Cultural Studies: Race, Gender, and Writing about Hip Hop." Some of the truths of this course are that "hip-hop dominates our cultural landscape, influencing everything from our music, to our fashion, to the very phrases we use to express ourselves," and that hip-hop has "mobilized the hyper-masculinity, mass consumerism, and heterosexism that reinforces the very culture it aims to challenge."

Meanwhile, "Cultural Studies: Comics and Graphic Medicine" asks, "How does the medium of comic books allow authors to craft new stories about health and illness?" For its part, "Sensational Feminisms" takes as truth that "the body is always politicized" and then asks, "How does the body feel when politicized?" This course is the *only* option if a Big Red student wants to read "transgender animal studies."

A more musically oriented student could take "Sounds, Sense, and Ideas: Who Run the World? Girls—Pop Music, Gender, and Media." To learn what "WAP" stands for is to understand the couture of the class:

> Is Cardi B and Megan Thee Stallion's "WAP" video
> an empowering anthem or an objectifying spectacle?

Can artists like Harry Styles and Bad Bunny truly "re-define" masculinity? This course asks how feminist or queer resistance might be possible within the mainstream pop music world. During our course, we will apply theoretical concepts from media studies and feminist, gender, and sexuality studies to critically analyze works by Madonna, Miley Cyrus, Beyoncé, Kim Petras, Lil Nas X, Britney Spears, and Missy Elliott (to name a few), with particular attention given to their use of mass media. Some theoretical topics to be discussed include appropriation, queer-baiting, post-feminism, and intersectionality.

A student who wants to avoid all such tendentiousness can skip straight to better courses.

One strong option is "Ithaca Bound: The *Odyssey* on Screen," in which students actually read a real classic of Western civilization and compare it to contemporary presentations of the story and its themes. The capstone project is a "mockup screenplay" of the student's own interpretation of the *Odyssey*, which the student pitches to the class.

A philosophically minded student might choose "Thinking and Thought: Dante's Examined Life." While reading Dante's *Inferno*, students consider, "Why do we study? What is the point of learning? Do we aspire to more than career success?"

A historically minded student might instead choose "The Fall of the Roman Empire" for experience with "close reading of a myriad of primary texts." Similarly, "Twilight of the Roman Republic: The Gracchi to Cleopatra" offers close encounters with Cicero, Caesar, and Sallust.

"Aspects of Medieval Culture: The Art of Friendship in the Latin Middle Ages" begins with Aristotle and Cicero on friendship and then shows how "the pagan inheritance took root in a Christian milieu." (In contrast, a myopic student of the period might choose "Medieval Crossdressings.")

Finally, a real student might choose "Philosophical Problems: Moral Relativism and Moral Skepticism." Wisely, "Our practical aim will be to learn to write as clearly as we think."

Foreign Language

Cornell students in the College of Arts and Sciences fulfill their foreign language requirement by completing either one intermediate-level course or eleven credits in any one foreign language (requiring two or three semesters in sequence). Cornell offers more than fifty languages, including twelve not taught by Cornell but offered through a collaborative arrangement with Columbia and Yale universities. Some languages do not meet the language requirement, so the number of Cornell-taught languages that meet the requirement (including languages such as Ukrainian, where only the elementary course is taught by Cornell) is thirty-two, plus American Sign Language.

The German courses in the Department of German Studies appear to be regular courses that teach German, unmarred by the ideological fads that have infected "German Studies" departments elsewhere.

Most other language courses also appear to be straight language courses, engaging texts and cultures. For better or worse, though, students experience more of a political edge in Advanced French. Their instruction in grammar "is integrated through a variety of topics such as social unrest and inequality, immigration crisis, social and geopolitical issues within and outside the Eurozone, post-Brexit . . . all chosen for thematic or cultural interest."

Students also can fulfill the requirement by taking Latin or Ancient Greek in the Department of Classics. Finally, the English Department helps students learn Old English, and the Africana Studies and Research Center helps students learn Quranic Arabic, although neither course counts for foreign language credit.

Distribution Requirements

Cornell undergraduates in the College of Arts and Sciences must take at least eight courses that collectively cover ten subject areas. They are grouped here for clarity under the headings of humanities/soft sciences and hard sciences.

HUMANITIES AND SOFT SCIENCES

- Arts, Literature, and Culture courses focus primarily on understanding "the complexities of the expression of the human condition" in social, cultural, and/or civilizational contexts.
- Ethics and the Mind can include psychology or linguistics besides philosophy. Courses on ethics "explore ways of reflecting on questions that concern the nature of justice, the good life, or human values in general."
- Social Difference is where to find the courses that focus on identity groups: "class, race, ethnicity, indigeneity, nationality, language, religion, gender, sexuality, and ability." This is also where students can learn Cornell faculty members' views about "how hierarchies in power and status shape social differences."
- Global Citizenship presumes that students have a "role as global citizens." This is where one finds progressive-oriented courses on topics such as "economic inequalities" and "environmental sustainability." Courses also can

focus on a particular part of the world.

- Historical Analysis is where to find the history courses but also many other disciplines with courses that offer little to no history despite meeting the history requirement.
- Social Sciences includes, as advertised, courses in the social sciences.

HARD SCIENCES

- Biological Sciences can include biology, genetics, biochemistry, or ecosystems.
- Physical Sciences is less about learning science than about scientific "enquiry": "an appreciation of how science generates and categorizes enduring knowledge of our physical world" so that "students will be better equipped to form opinions on scientific issues that affect the world."
- Statistics and Data Science focus on "data literacy" and develop a critical approach to statistics.
- Symbolic and Mathematical Reasoning courses can include math, logic, modeling, algorithms and quantitative methods, and quantitative reasoning.

Here are some standout courses in each area—courses to take or to avoid. Not all courses are available each year. Selections are generally from the Spring 2024 semester, so noteworthy options available only in other semesters may not appear here.

ARTS, LITERATURE, AND CULTURE

Among hundreds of options in Arts, Literature, and Culture, here are some of the least worthwhile from an academic perspective.

- Videogames in East and Southeast Asia: Dressed up as

more, it addresses "the factors that regionalize videogames as a cultural imagination and an industrial system in East and Southeast Asia."

- Gender and Sexuality in Southeast Asian Cinema: "Current writings in feminism, Buddhist studies, affect theory, queer studies, postcolonial theory, and film studies."
- Beyoncé Nation: The Remix: all the Beyhive you wanted and more.
- Whiteness in Literature and Popular Culture: This course begins with "the violent events in Charlottesville in 2017" and "the January 6th insurrection at the US Capitol in 2021."
- Black Holes: Races and the Cosmos: "The fundamentals of astronomy concepts through readings in Black Studies."
- Punk Rock Feminism Rules: Riot Grrrl, Community Building, and the Archive: This course tells the story of this subculture's efforts "to create a safer, more equitable punk scene" and includes, on a more academic note, archival methods.
- Of Bodies and Flesh: Black, Indigenous, and Women of Color Feminisms: This course will "contemplate flesh and bodies as multiply symbolic of land, labor, sovereignty, and reproduction, while also impossibly representative of anything beyond the physical and material. Engaging both scholarly and creative work, we will explore texts located in feminist studies, queer and trans studies, critical and comparative ethnic studies, and disability studies."
- Thinking about History with the Manson Murders: It's a quite narrow option.

Serious students can take the following, among others. Shakespeare has not entirely disappeared, nor has the English survey course.

- The Greek Experience: "Among our texts will be Homer's *Odyssey*, Greek lyric poetry, the tragedians,

Aristophanes, Plato, and Lucian, set against a backdrop of Greek geography, history, and art."

- Spinoza and the New Spinozism: This course addresses fundamental human questions philosophically.
- Shakespeare's *Hamlet*: The Seminar: A close reading of the play.
- Literatures in English I: From Old English to the New World: "Here's a chance to study some of the greatest hits of the literary tradition in a single semester: *Beowulf*; Arthurian legends; works by Chaucer, Shakespeare, Anne Bradstreet, Ben Franklin, Sageyowatha [eighteenth-century Seneca chief, and] Phillis Wheatley."
- *Beowulf*: The course uses a bilingual edition "so that students may read in Old and Modern English."
- Milton: Political Revolution and *Paradise Lost*: "Was Milton a revolutionary poet?" The course focuses on "how Milton reconciled the dual imperatives to resist illegitimate rule and to obey true authority."
- Classical Tradition: The course tracks aspects of the legacies of ancient Greece and Rome through the centuries.

ETHICS AND THE MIND

Students can do very well choosing an Ethics and the Mind option—or they can choose poorly. Here are some highlights and lowlights among thirty-four choices in Spring 2024.

LOWLIGHTS:

- Introduction to Critical Theory wears its politics on its *culottes*: "Shortly after the 2016 election, *The New Yorker* published an article entitled 'The Frankfurt School Knew Trump was Coming.' . . . [T]he Frankfurt School played a pivotal role in . . . analyses of authoritarianism and democracy [and in] critiques of capitalism."

- What Is a People? The Social Contract and Its Discontents opens with Jean-Jacques Rousseau's "revolutionary" focus on the "general will" of "the people" and applies it to "the crisis of political representation" and "the forms of the social contract to which they have given rise. Our discussions will range from major political events (the French and Haitian Revolutions, the Paris Commune, colonialism and decolonization, May '68) to contemporary debates around universalism, secularism, immigration, and 'marriage for all.' Readings by Rousseau, Robespierre, L'Ouverture, Michelet, Marx, Freud, Arendt, Balibar, and Rancière."
- Iroquoian Linguistics is very narrow for a general education course, focusing on Northern Iroquoian linguistics. The course has no discernible relationship to ethics or the mind. Linguistics is a fascinating field in itself but generally does not fit this subject area.
- Introduction to Acting is even more of a stretch. Procrustes could make it fit only at a great cost. The correct one-word response: Macbeth.

HIGHLIGHTS:

- Civil Disobedience is particularly relevant and thought-provoking for students in a post–October 7 environment.
- Better Decisions for Life, Love, and Money features "a team of psychologists and economists" who use research to help students learn how to "make sound decisions," recognize "common biases," "critically evaluate empirical evidence," and evaluate the likely effectiveness of policy proposals.
- Choices and Consequences in Computing examines the "societal challenges" of "digital technology" with the goal of preparing students to think ethically about future situations. (Ethical Issues in Engineering Practice is a narrower course that also gets one's ethical gears moving.)

- Moral Dilemmas in the Law exposes students to the actual text of Supreme Court cases as students consider foundational moral questions about America's system of government.
- Developmental Psychology is a standard content-rich introductory course.
- Early Modern Philosophy appears to rotate through different courses in "advanced study of a central concept, problem, or figure in seventeenth- to eighteenth-century philosophy." Students focused on Spinoza's *Ethics* in Spring 2024. (Students also can take courses in medieval philosophy, twentieth-century philosophy, or modern political philosophy to meet the requirement.)
- Religion and Reason uses philosophy to investigate the theological idea of God as a perfect being.

SOCIAL DIFFERENCE

With such a crowded field of identity groups, each making its case, it can be hard for a student to decide which oppression to pay tuition to learn about.

- Asian American: Topics include "war and empire; queer and feminist lives and histories . . . anti-Asian violence; settler colonialism, and postcolonial critique."
- Indigenous: "Critical responses to and forms of resistance toward neocolonial political and economic agendas . . . the history of victimization of indigenous peoples through colonial oppression . . . the complex interconnectivity between the ecological and the sociocultural," and more.
- Latino: "The politics of resistance and solidarity of Latinxs/Hispanics in North America, with a primary focus on the US political system. . . . [C]onceptual categorizations and definitions of the Latina/o/x population, pondering whether Latin@s should be regarded as a racial or

ethnic group. Then, we follow with a historical survey of Latino migration to the US and analyze how interlocking systems of oppression shape the material conditions and lived experiences of Latin@/x people. Ultimately, we conclude by analyzing Latino collective action to understand how they organize at the local, national, and transnational levels to confront systems of inequality . . . [including] neoliberalism."

- Immigrants: "Central to this class is the exploration of multiple systems of marginalization that shape the opportunities, material conditions, and lived experiences of immigrants in the US. We conclude with an exploration of historical and contemporary migrant-led forms of resistance, such as the Immigrant Rights Movement, and its linkages to other transnational struggles for social justice."
- Palestinians: "We will learn about Palestinian life—in Palestine, exile, and diaspora—and ask what these experiences can teach us about colonialism, indigeneity, capitalism, and resistance."
- Intersectional Disability Studies: The course title says it all.
- Deaf Americans: "Oppression of signed languages," among other topics.
- South Asian religions: "The [modern] impact of colonialism, nationalism, and globalization."
- Race in America generally: "Race has been the terrain on which competing ideas of the American nation have been contested."
- Women: "We will . . . consider how larger structural systems of both privilege and oppression affect individuals' identities, experiences, and options." (This is a typical introductory gender studies course.)
- Trans Studies: "The vexed relation between queer theory and Trans Studies . . . the specific violence faced by Black trans women and the possibility that Blackness itself might be para-ontologically trans," and so on. (Note that

the Gender and the Brain course, for its part, takes the sex binary as a given and does not take sides between these two genders.)

- The French: The French Studies Program offers some different ways to learn about oppression in the course French and Francophone Literature and Culture, including a section on "women and sexual minorities" and one on "colonialism and the other." This course also counts for the foreign language requirement.
- The Germans: The course Changing Worlds: Migration, Minorities, and German Literature gives special attention to "Jews, Turks, and Black Germans," with less attention to "other minorities."
- The Spanish: The course Fashion Victims treats "such topics as textile trade and Spanish empire, ethnicity and national garb, fashion and gender norms, as well as contemporary debates around cultural appropriation."

Then there are some anthropology courses, including:

- Economy, Power, and Inequality: "What social, political, environmental, and religious values underlie different forms of economic organization? And how do they produce racial, ethnic, class, gender, and sexual inequalities? This course uses ... formalism, substantivism, Marxist and feminist theory, critical race studies, and science and technology studies." One might guess how the discussion of "capitalism and socialism" is intended to turn out.
- Embodiment of Inequality: A Bioarchaeological Perspective: "A deep archaeological perspective on the lived experience of inequality and the historically contingent nature of sexuality, gender, and violence. . . . We will not only consider privilege and marginalization in lived experience, but also in death, examining how unequal social relationships are reproduced when the dead body is colonized as an object of study."

Is there a way out? Yes. The philosophy courses Moral Dilemmas in the Law, and Topics in Twentieth-Century Philosophy, seem most likely to avoid taking identity-group oppression for granted. Also, Shi'ism: Poetics and Politics simply teaches about Shi'ism in a "socio-political context." It appears to be silent about oppression by or against this major world religion (which seems like a missed opportunity in the context of the Social Difference requirement). Here are some other possible options:

- One partial way out is to take a literature course that meets the requirement. For example, the English Department has one on nineteenth-century Gothic literature—but beware—this course still includes "scathing critiques . . . of the monstrous underlying grand sentiments of American Exceptionalism" to ensure students get enough anti-Americanism for this distribution requirement. (The other English Department course meeting the requirement is Critical Approaches to Video Games. Avoid the opportunity "to consider how race, gender, indigeneity, and sexuality shape the code and the machines that we play" by reading "scholars in Indigenous studies, Black feminism, and video game studies.") In French one could take Bankers, Gamblers, [and] Hustlers to critique capitalism via well-known and less-known French authors.
- Another possible escape is into Magic and Witchcraft in the Greco-Roman World, but the course cannot help but include "social class, gender, religion, and ethnic and cultural identity" in order to fit.
- Reading between the lines, one might infer that the course Of Saints, Poets, and Revolutionaries: Medieval and Modern Iran and Central Asia is mostly about culture and that it just throws a bone to the Social Difference requirement by including the words "colonial and post-colonial occupations" in the course description. Similarly, the course Nobody Expects the Spanish

Inquisition: Inquisitors, Heretics, and Truth in the Early Modern World looks more like a history course that sneaked into the Social Difference area through the theme of heresy.

- Introduction to Anthropological Theory might work out if one believes that anthropological theory is still politically neutral.
- Music and Sound Studies is a discordant choice in Social Difference, but at least it gives the Department of Music a chance to score some tuition.

GLOBAL CITIZENSHIP

The distribution requirement called Global Citizenship is often just a different flavor of Social Difference. Indeed, some Cornell courses meet either requirement. Here are some noteworthy courses, starting with the less serious.

- Heat Waves and Global Health: Environmental Justice and Social Autopsy in London and Beyond: "A collaborative, intensive examination of the growing problem of extreme heat for global health and urban environmental justice," including a spring break visit to London.
- Caribbean Worlds: Landscape, Labor, and Climate Imaginaries: A seminar course "interpreting the industrialized-urbanized ecological territory in terms of 'capitalist ruination' which, nonetheless, holds possibilities for other modes of environmentality, as the hazards effected by climate change fundamentally disrupt and transform the very urbanity constituted through colonial and later resource extractive appropriations."
- Cayuga Language and Culture: An understandable course given Cornell's location and history, but this course does little over the span of a year. The spring term continues "with a focus on plants and growing in the spring."

On the serious list:

- China's Next Economy: "An analytical framework to understand China's ongoing economic transformation." Other courses on China look fact-rich, too. Likewise, consider The History and Politics of Modern Egypt.
- Introduction to Comparative Government and Politics: A regular political science course.
- Political Violence: "The causes and consequences of modern-day civil wars."
- The Viking Age: Scandinavian history over the years 800–1100.
- History of State and Society in Modern Iran: Through Literature and Film, and The Ottoman Empire 1800–1922: Both courses offer what they advertise.
- Modern Spanish Survey: An introduction to literature in general and modern Spanish literature in particular. It also meets the foreign language requirement.

HISTORICAL ANALYSIS

Again, this area overlaps with subject areas above, with some courses listed under multiple areas. While many courses are very narrow, that is no impediment to learning how to engage in historical analysis. Until Cornell produces real requirements to learn American history and the history of Western civilization at the college level, this area will continue to be just another distribution requirement.

Among courses not yet mentioned, here are some to avoid:

- Fighting for Our Lives: Black Women's Reproductive Health and Activism in Historical Perspective: "Deeply inspired by the field of Black Feminist Health Science Studies, a field that advocates for the centrality of activism in healthcare . . . this course examines how issues

of gender, race, class, ability, and power intersect . . . .
Ultimately, this course will yield a deeper understanding of how Black women have transformed existential
and literal threats on their lives into a robust terrain of
community-based activism and a movement for reproductive justice."

- Comparative Modernities: This seminar invokes "the
  effects of capitalism . . . and the onset of neoliberal globalization" to study art "in a global context."
- Reading Race: Early Modern Art: "This seminar will critically explore constructions of Blackness, whiteness, and
  racialized 'otherness' and will consider the roles played
  by art and material culture in practices of race-making.
  Thinking materially, students assess the impact of different artistic media on understandings of racialized difference. Considering race at its intersections with gender,
  class, religion, science, and disability" (and so on).
- Liquidities: Seascapes in Art and as History: "We will explore the methodological potential [that] watery thinking offers for an art history attuned to cross currents,
  fluid interactions, and unsettled narratives" and will
  challenge "the limitations inherent in the terrestrial bias
  of much Western scholarship."
- Disasters! A History of Colonial Failures in the Atlantic
  World, 1450–1750: "Why did some colonies fail and other
  thrived? What role did social factors like gender, race,
  and class play in colonial failures? What can we learn
  about colonialism and imperialism through a focus on
  when those processes ended in disasters?"
- The Revolutionary as Author: Autobiography and Political Myth: Autobiographies of "leftist political figures"
  with, inevitably, "special attention to the question[s] of
  gender, ethnicity, religion, and race."
- Costume Construction Studio: "Draping and patterning
  basics . . . basic machine sewing experience helpful, but

not required." Such a bad fit, one would think it's a mistake, but it slips in by including "historic silhouettes."

Here are some courses to take:

- The US and the Middle East: This course appears to be an objective account of events from the 1800s on. Also consider Introduction to Judaism.
- Romanesque and Early Gothic Art and Architecture: Europe and the Mediterranean, 1000–1150 AD: Monumental, though it's more about culture than particular historical events.
- Medieval Romance: Voyages to the Otherworld: A real course in European literature. Or take the Chaucer course, reading it in Middle English. Or take the *Beowulf* course using a bilingual edition. Or take the fascinating course on Tolstoy, a man of contradictions. There is hope for literature students at Cornell!
- The Making of Modern Europe, from 1500 to the Present: A sincere attempt to teach a broad survey of European history and make it relevant to today.

Finally, special mention is warranted for this course on China, named Global Maoism: History and Present. Here is the course description:

> Maoism and Chinese Communism are not history after Mao's death in 1976. In China, Maoism holds the key to the enduring success of the Chinese Communist Party (CCP), one of the most remarkable organizations of the twentieth and twenty-first centuries that has survived the collapse of communism in Europe and the USSR. With the beneficial transformation brought by capitalism and globalization in China, the end of the Cold War and the narrative of the "end of history" cannot explain the resurgence of Maoism.

Is the course merely descriptive, or is it celebratory, or is it a warning? From the description alone, one cannot tell. That suggests a worthwhile course.

SOCIAL SCIENCES

The social "sciences" comprise a broad set of disciplines, which offer courses that may have little to no quantitative analysis as in the hard sciences or statistics. Nevertheless, students can choose courses well or poorly to meet this requirement.

Choosing poorly:

- Cages and Creativity: Arts in Incarceration: Learning "how and why art is taught in prisons" and art's role in recidivism and reentry are not worth the tuition to meet the social sciences requirement.
- Heat Waves and Global Health: Listed above.
- Intersectional Disability Studies: Listed above.

Choosing well means focusing on economics or one of the better political science courses:

- The Nature, Functions, and Limits of Law: A serious political science "general education course to acquaint students with how our legal system pursues the goals of society. The course introduces students to various perspectives on the nature of law, what functions it ought to serve in society, and what it can and cannot accomplish. The course proceeds in the belief that such matters constitute a valuable and necessary part of a general education, not only for pre-law students but especially for students in other fields."
- Other courses in political science (Department of Government) or American Studies also look good on paper, including The American Presidency (working from the twentieth century on), Congress and the Legislative

Process, and Introduction to Political Theory.

- Introductory Microeconomics: A standard high-value course on "how the price system operates in determining what goods are produced, how goods are produced, who receives income, and how the price system is modified and influenced by private organizations and government policy." Preferable to Introductory Macroeconomics, which is fine and also looks like the standard course. Intermediate Micro and Macro, the econometrics courses, and most of the rest of the Economics Department's choices also fulfill the requirement well.

- Research Methods: Design and Measurement: For anyone planning to pursue further social science research.

- Better Decisions for Life, Love, and Money, and China's Next Economy: Both are listed above.

BIOLOGICAL SCIENCES AND PHYSICAL SCIENCES

While it is easy for students to choose poorly in the humanities, social sciences, and identity disciplines at Cornell, the hard sciences do not have this problem in their general education options. This means that when professors consider how to improve the science curriculum, they can spend more time on interesting questions of pedagogy and how to make lab sessions meaningful.

Even so, the overall critique of distribution requirements applies here: Is it enough to learn to think a little like a biologist or a physical scientist, or is there general information about biology and other fields that every educated Cornell graduate should know? Does it matter that one student learns about the hippocampus while another learns about animal communication, but neither learns anything about microbiology? Does it matter that one Cornell student learns about the solar system while another learns some chemistry, a third learns how to use ocean satellite remote sensing data, and a fourth learns about electronic circuits?

Almost every course meeting the biological sciences requirement looks like a real biology course that helps students think like a biologist (broadly including biochemists, ecologists, and other specialists). Similarly, every course in the physical sciences looks like a course a humanities major would be proud to complete with a B-minus, were it not for grade inflation.

Unfortunately, one course is a distraction from that strong showing. Natural History of the Magic Kingdom: Understanding Animal Behavior through Animated Films looks like it was designed for members of Cornell's athletics teams who want to watch *Finding Nemo*. Indeed, the course carries a special note: "Course is suitable for non–life science students."

In the physical sciences, it appears that Our Solar System is the best analog to the historic "Rocks for Jocks," being taught in ten sections in Spring 2024.

STATISTICS AND DATA SCIENCE: SYMBOLIC AND MATHEMATICAL REASONING

A large number of Cornell students take Introduction to Statistics. The Spring 2024 lecture course was divided into twenty-five sections. It's probably the least challenging way to complete the requirement in statistics and data science among a few dozen challenging options. But it doesn't look easy. Further kudos to Cornell for keeping standards high in the hard sciences.

The courses available in symbolic and mathematical reasoning deserve the same respect. The two Introduction to Computing courses had a total of twenty-five sections in Spring 2024 and might be the least challenging courses in this area, but they look like no walk in the park on a climate-change field trip to London. The economics course on game theory also meets this requirement.

Almost everything else looks both really hard and really worthwhile—unless one is never going to use advanced math in the future, but then there would be no good reason to take, say, Matrix Groups.

Conclusion

Here's what an enterprising slacker could take at Cornell to meet all general education requirements, provided that the courses are offered and available in the right order, and not considering the possibility of taking eight instead of ten core courses due to the ability to double-count a course. (Most students, even slackers, must also take physical education and swimming or test out.)

Slacker Curriculum:

WRITING AND FOREIGN LANGUAGE

- Queer Girlhood
- Sounds, Sense, and Ideas: Who Run the World? Girls—Pop Music, Gender, and Media
- French

HUMANITIES AND SOFT SCIENCES

- Punk Rock Feminism Rules: Riot Grrrl, Community Building, and the Archive
- Introduction to Critical Theory
- Intersectional Disability Studies
- Heat Waves and Global Health: Environmental Justice and Social Autopsy in London and Beyond
- Costume Construction Studio
- Cages and Creativity: Arts in Incarceration

HARD SCIENCES

- Natural History of the Magic Kingdom: Understanding Animal Behavior through Animated Films
- Our Solar System
- Introduction to Statistics
- Introduction to Computing: A Design and Development Perspective

Striver Curriculum:

WRITING AND FOREIGN LANGUAGE

- Thinking and Thought: Dante's Examined Life
- Twilight of the Roman Republic: The Gracchi to Cleopatra
- Ancient Greek

HUMANITIES AND SOFT SCIENCES

- Literatures in English I: From Old English to the New World
- Better Decisions for Life, Love, and Money
- Moral Dilemmas in the Law
- Modern Political Philosophy
- The Making of Modern Europe, from 1500 to the Present
- The American Presidency (or Introductory Micro-economics)

HARD SCIENCES

- General Microbiology Lectures (with lab)
- Physics I: Mechanics and Heat
- Probability Models and Inference for the Social Sciences
- Modeling with Calculus for the Life Sciences

YALE UNIVERSITY

U ndergraduates of Yale College must fulfill distributional and skills requirements in order to
graduate, in addition to the credits required to
complete a major. Yale's "distributional" approach means
that there are no mandated courses of study for students.
Rather, undergraduates are free to choose from hundreds
of course offerings to fulfill each general requirement,
with topics that run the gamut from serious to frivolous.
As a result, the quality of a Yale education can vary wildly. While a student choosing well could receive a strong
liberal arts education, one could also graduate from Yale
without having studied the liberal arts in any meaningful
sense of the term.

Yale presents its distributional requirements as a
means of ensuring that students "learn about a variety
of subjects and intellectual approaches" while also developing "certain foundational skills—writing, quantitative
reasoning, and language competency—that hold the key
to opportunities in later study and later life." To ensure
the former, Yale requires each student to take at least two
course credits in the social sciences, two in the humanities and arts, and two in the sciences. To develop the
latter, students must take at least two course credits in
quantitative reasoning, two in writing, and one to three
in a foreign language. Since the vast majority of Yale's

undergraduate courses fulfill one course credit, the distributional requirements typically take at least eleven courses to complete.

SOCIAL SCIENCES

Yale defines social science as the study of "human social behavior and networks using a variety of methodologies and both qualitative and quantitative analysis" and offers hundreds of options across roughly forty disciplines to fulfill this area requirement. The college expects the requirement to help students "appreciate the perspective of the other as well as the particularities of society" and develop a "nuanced sense of the world around them," thereby preparing them for "lives of civic engagement."

Unfortunately, most of the course options available suggest that by "civic engagement," Yale means political activism, and that by "nuanced sense," it means one informed by identity politics. Consider the following:

- Managing Blackness in "White Space": Defining "white space" as a "perceptual category that assumes a particular space to be predominately white," the course "explores the challenge black people face when managing their lives in this white space."
- Comparative Settler Geographies: "How do Indigenous and/or occupied peoples contest settler cartographies through placemaking and other strategies?" Case studies include South Africa, Morocco/Western Sahara, Israel/Palestine, and China/Tibet.
- American Exceptionalism: "This class takes a critical look at the ideology of American exceptionalism . . . . Students explore how the *1619 Project*, dinosaur paleontology, and the Broadway musical *Hamilton* are rooted in ideologies of American exceptionalism and why Indigenous groups say Mount Rushmore, Thanksgiving, and native-themed

sports mascots are celebrations of genocide .... This course, therefore, invites students to re-think their national attachments, investments, allegiances, and fantasies and to consider the circumstances that led Audre Lorde to say, 'We are citizens of a country that stands upon the wrong side of every liberation struggle on earth.'"

- Racial Power and the US Supreme Court: "This course explores the ways that contemporary decisions of the US Supreme Court reflect an enduring commitment to the political project of racial hierarchy and racial power."

- US Militarism and Popular Culture explores America's "growing culture" of militarism, studying its manifestation across pop culture phenomena, including *American Idol*, Starbucks, baking competitions, reality TV, *Iron Man*, *Captain Marvel*, and the Kansas City Chiefs.

- Race and Place in British New Wave, K-Pop, and Beyond: Where "racial, regional, and national identities" meet pop music.

- Climate Privilege: A Sophomore Seminar: A class on climate "privilege, complicity, and complacency."

- The Politics of Crime and Punishment in American Cities: Topics include "sentencing algorithms," "felon (dis)enfranchisement," "stop-and-frisk," and "police use of force."

- The Media and Democracy: A course examining how journalists "hold power to account." Course materials consist of case studies "from nineteenth-century yellow journalism to the #MeToo and #BlackLivesMatter movements, to the January 6 Capitol attack and the advent of AI journalism."

- Contesting Injustice: The course description makes no mention of the contested meanings of justice and injustice, instead focusing on "why, when, and how people organize collectively to challenge political, social, and economic injustice," as well as "the extent, causes, and consequences of inequality."

- Place, Race, and Memory in Schools: "Given the weight that narratives of social mobility in the United States place upon education, there is profound interest in the roles that schools play in perpetuating racial disparities in American society and the opportunities that education writ large might provide for remedying them."
- Sports and Society: In this course, "we center gender and race in order to understand how sport serves as a contested social terrain that both reproduces and challenges systems of patriarchy and racism."
- Psychology of Gender: Topics include "gender hierarchy," the "gender binary," and the "cis-hetero-patriarchal family unit."

Serious students do have a few good options. These include several solid economics courses, including courses on American Economic History and the History of Economic Thought. Yale's Program on Ethics, Politics, and Economics (EP&E) also offers a number of substantive options, such as:

- Classics [of] Justice, Morality, and the State, in which students "explore how some of the most influential thinkers in Western philosophy, politics, and economics answered the following questions, 'How should we live?' 'How can I be virtuous?' 'What makes actions right or wrong?' 'What is justice and what makes society just?'" and more.
- Classics of EP&E—Intellectual Origins of Liberalism and Conservatism, in which "discussions and readings confront liberal and conservative perspectives on human nature; reason; freedom; tradition; individual rights; religion; the Enlightenment; market economies; democratic participation; and equality."
- Philosophy of Science for the Study of Politics, which considers "the ways in which assumptions about science influence models of political behavior."

Other highlights include:

- Directed Studies seminars on the History of Political Thought, in which readings draw from Herodotus, Thucydides, Plato, Aristotle, Augustine, and Aquinas, in the fall, and Machiavelli, Hobbes, Locke, Rousseau, Burke, Tocqueville, Emerson, Marx, Nietzsche, and Arendt, in the spring.
- Foundations of Modern Social Theory, which focuses on "major works of social thought from the beginning of the modern era through the 1900s," including W. E. B. Du Bois, Simone De Beauvoir, Adam Smith, Thomas Hobbes, Jean-Jacques Rousseau, Immanuel Kant, Emile Durkheim, Max Weber, and Karl Marx.
- Lincoln's Statecraft and Rhetoric, a course that undertakes a "close reading of major speeches and letters" by Lincoln and examines the "ways in which his vision of American democracy both drew upon and transformed the founders' vision."

HUMANITIES AND ARTS

Yale defines courses in the humanities and arts as those that examine "how we chronicle and interpret the expression of human experience," and it offers hundreds of options across almost sixty disciplines to fulfill this area requirement. Yale expects this requirement to cultivate "appreciation for the past," develop "insight into the experiences of others," foster "tolerance for ambiguity," and hone "sophisticated analytical skills that provide essential preparation for careers in most areas of contemporary life." Ultimately, Yale concludes, the humanities and arts should teach "understanding and appreciation of the highest achievements of humanity."

Yale lists 751 course options to fulfill the humanities and arts requirement in the fall semester of 2024, more than one third of the 1,899 courses listed in the Yale College catalogue, though neither number filters out cross-listings. This makes the humanities and arts requirement very loose—if a Yale College class outside of the STEM fields interests a student, there's an almost 50 percent chance it also fulfills the humanities and arts requirement.

Here are some of the least worthwhile from an academic perspective.

- "I Don't Like to Argue": The Styles and Politics of Humility is the ultimate safe space, where argument itself is avoided for its "power relations and tonal effects" and students instead experiment with "alternative styles of knowing."
- Decolonizing the Mind explores "the effects of colonialism and post-colonial power relations" on the field of psychiatry, posing questions such as, "Is reason singular, plural, or culturally bound or universal?" and "To what extent is spiritual possession a rational experience?"
- Feminism without Women: Modernist and Postcolonial Textual Experiments, true to its name, draws on texts and theories that "put pressure on the very category of 'woman' as they strive to rethink feminism as a non-identitarian world-making project."
- Paper: Material and Medium "sets out to challenge our understanding of paper as a neutral or passive bearer of inscriptions" by "uncover[ing] paper's status as a commodity bound up in a complex web of economic processes, as an instrument of political power, as a gendered and racialized object, and as a material that can be cut, shuffled, and even eaten."
- Nighttime: The Night in History tells the story of discrimination against nighttime, examining the "roots of the prejudice against darkness," the "reasons why we fear the night," and the "process of criminalization, commercialization, and even politicization of nocturnal spaces."

- Drink Culture: The History, Ethics, and Aesthetics of Cocktails examines "how drink culture itself is bound up with colonialism, imperialism, the rise of science, and the commodification of art."
- Introduction to the Occult Sciences provides a "comparative history of the occult sciences from antiquity to the present." Topics range from astrology and alchemy to "recipes for summoning demons and angels."
- Words, Words, Words: The Structure and History of English Words explores the "wonderful world of words," from "ain't" and "eerily," to "meggings" and "bae." Texts include works of Shakespeare as well as "anonymous online bloggers."
- "None Dare Call It Conspiracy:" Paranoia and Conspiracy Theories in Twentieth- and Twenty-first-century America considers anti-Semitism as a "foundational form of conspiracy theorizing" but also pays particular attention to the "role of conspiracy theories in far-right politics, ranging from the John Birch Society in the 1960s to the Tea Party, QAnon, and beyond in the twenty-first century."
- Beyoncé Makes History: Black Radical Tradition History, Culture, Theory, and Politics through Music "traces the relationship between Beyoncé's artistic genius and Black intellectual practice."
- Country Music in America: the greatest hits.
- Pop Sapphism surveys the "lesbian presence in pop" culture, "from figures like K-Stew (Kristen Stewart), Janelle Monáe, and a slew of 'converted' reality contestants, to the controversies surrounding 'Gaylorism' itself."
- War Games: where video games meet "political violence (both real and imaginary) in a global and post-Cold War context."
- East Asian Martial Arts Films: a rather narrow option.
- Embodied Methods: Lessons in Praxis from Women of Color: "Understanding ethnic studies, black studies, and

gender studies as necessarily anti-disciplinary practices, this course explores modes of research that embrace the body as a tool, a way of knowing, and a method for cutting across the silos and boundaries that academic disciplines impose."

In blinding contrast, serious students can choose any of the following rigorous courses in English, philosophy, and political science, among others:

- Directed Studies seminars offer "a select group of first-year students an intense interdisciplinary introduction to some of the seminal texts of Western and Near East cultures." Literature seminar readings draw from Homer, Aeschylus, Sophocles, Virgil, the Bible, and Dante, in the fall, and Petrarch, Cervantes, Shakespeare, Milton, Wordsworth, Goethe, Tolstoy, Proust, and Eliot, in the spring, while Philosophy seminar readings focus on Plato and Aristotle in the fall and Descartes, Hume, Kant, and Nietzsche in the spring.
- Thucydides: A close reading of Thucydides's *History of the Peloponnesian War*, considering "the psychological and structural causes of war, the relation of justice to necessity, the susceptibility of democracy to imperialism and demagoguery, and the experience of war itself."
- Nature and Human Nature features "close study of three classic texts: Galileo's *Dialogue Concerning the Two Chief World Systems* (1632), Giambattista Vico's *New Science* (1744), and Darwin's *Origin of Species* (1859)—fundamental texts locating humans in the cosmos, in society, and in natural history, respectively."
- Readings in English Poetry I and II introduce students to the English literary tradition, from Chaucer, Milton, and Shakespeare to Wordsworth, Yeats, and Eliot.
- Individualism and Community: Tocqueville and J. S. Mill compares the political philosophies of Tocqueville and

Mill, "asking how each understood the relations between individualism and community, democracy and liberty, and citizenship and human flourishing."

- Six Pretty Good Interior Journeys, part of Yale's "Six Pretty Good Ideas" first-year seminar series, examines "the journey within" in texts by Augustine of Hippo, Teresa of Avila, Frederick Douglass, Black Elk, and Mahatma Gandhi.
- The Mortality of the Soul: From Aristotle to Heidegger "explores fundamental philosophical questions of the relation between matter and form, life and spirit, [and] necessity and freedom" in the works of Aristotle, Heidegger, and contemporary philosophers.
- Tragedy in the European Literary Tradition: "Works might include Aristotle's *Poetics* or Homer's *Iliad* and plays by Aeschylus, Sophocles, Euripides, Seneca, [and] Shakespeare," among others.

SCIENCES

Yale defines science as "the study of the principles of the physical and the natural world through observation and experimentation" and expects "close study of a science" to equip students "to evaluate natural phenomena and the opinions of experts, and to make, understand, and evaluate arguments about them." The goal here is for students to develop the "scientific literacy" that belongs to "educated citizens."

For the most part, the 217 course listings to fulfill the science requirement demand the actual study of a science. In doing so, they should familiarize students with the methods and principles of modern science. With course topics ranging from archeology to psychology, however, it's hard to see how the requirement guarantees scientific literacy—the basic content knowledge necessary to understand and evaluate scientific arguments and nonspecialist scientific literature.

More concerning are the course options that do not demand substantial study of a science. Serious students should avoid classes on the politics of science, including:

- Asian Americans and STEM, a first-year seminar "to explore the ways in which scientific practice has been shaped by US histories of imperialism and colonialism, migration and racial exclusion, domestic and international labor and economics, and war."
- Current Issues in Medicine and Public Health, which concerns "issues in public health and medicine that get extensive media attention and provoke policy debates," with a "prime focus" on "vaccination attitudes."
- Biology, the World, and Us: "This course is for non-science majors who wish to gain an understanding of modern biology by examining the scientific basis of current issues" such as "the climate crisis" and the "new green revolution."
- The Science and Politics of HIV/AIDS, which considers "the potential harm of conspiracy theories based on false science" and "how stigmas associated with poverty, gender inequality, sexual preference, and race facilitate an ongoing epidemic."

LANGUAGE AND QUANTITATIVE REASONING

Yale's skills requirements in language and quantitative reasoning appear to be the most straightforward of all the distributional requirements. Language options consist in language courses, while quantitative reasoning options consist in STEM courses.

Yale encourages knowledge of more than one language through its skills requirement for a few reasons. Familiarity with more than one language can result in "heightened sophistication in the use of one's own language; unmediated access to texts otherwise available only in translation, or not at all; and the ability to recognize and cross cultural barriers." To that end, Yale offers more than seventy-five languages to fulfill this requirement, ranging from Akkadian to Zulu.

Yale's skills requirement in quantitative reasoning, for its part, aims to equip graduates with basic tools in mathematics and statistics to "use quantitative information to make, understand, and evaluate arguments." To that end, Yale offers courses in Mathematics, Statistics and Data Science, Computer Science, Economics, Engineering and Applied Science, Astronomy, Chemistry, Earth and Planetary Sciences, Linguistics, Music, Philosophy, and Physics. All courses appear to require rigorous quantitative reasoning. Still, a student looking for an easy way out can opt for Approaches to International Development, in which topics include "institutions and colonialism; social capital; inequality; migration and forced displacement; rural finance and labor markets; and gender." Otherwise, the quantitative reasoning requirement may be Yale's most robust.

WRITING

Yale offers 298 courses that may fulfill its writing requirement, 264 of which carry one or more of the other distributional designations, although Yale specifies that "a single course may be applied to only one distributional requirement." Yale expects the writing requirement to help students "develop the ability to express more nuanced thought and intellectual practices that distinguish active from passive learners." What distinguishes writing-designated courses from others is not that they require more writing, however, but that "they provide more help with writing assignments." At Yale, this means that writing-designated courses are characterized by methods such as "learning from model essays," receiving "detailed feedback," and "reviewing writing in small groups."

Among the many options offered to fulfill the writing requirement are those that do not seem particularly writing-focused, such as lab courses in biology and chemistry, an introductory course in electronics, and a course about dance on film, in which the only assignment mentioned is "an original short film for a final class project." For an "inquiry into the ways that performance rips open language, rendering words at once more capacious and more ambiguous," students can opt for a theater course on "experimental writing and performance."

Also of note are writing seminars taught by the English Department, with a wealth of DEI-infused topics to choose from, including:

- Asian Plasticities, which considers "Asian and Asian American artworks as a site for thinking about race, beauty, and authenticity, as well as the ways in which empire, capital, and colonialism have cut up and remolded the globe like a giant, scalpel-wielding hand."
- Black and Indigenous Ecologies: an opportunity to "engage with anti-colonial and anti-racist attempts to craft an image of the earth no longer made in the ecocidal image of imperialist Western man (or the *anthropos* of 'Anthropocene'), and to imagine a future to be held and composed in common by all."
- Home: a study in "how home overlaps with spirituality, language politics, hierarchies of gender and labor, and educational opportunities, and how climate crises, pandemics, global economics, and immigration policies impact home."
- Monstrosity and the Vampire: Through "critical texts such as Susan Stryker's 'My Words to Victor Frankenstein Above the Village of Chamounix: Performing Transgender Rage' and Jack Halberstam's *The Queer Art of Failure*, the vampire in its various iterations across time and medium, will help us to think about mechanisms of,

and resistance against, colonialism, capitalism, heteronormativity, compulsory ablebodiedness, [and] racism."

- On Disability: "In this course, you will learn to write
  thoughtfully and inclusively about topics of disability
  justice, to read texts about disability and diagnosis with
  an eye for bias and prejudice, and to research and argue
  points about equity, access, and liberation."
- Pirates: "Through discussion, writing, and other activities, we will interrogate what popular depictions of
  pirates can reveal about perspectives on history, issues
  of empire, race, gender and sexuality, attitudes towards
  work and citizenship, questions of genre in entertainment, and more."
- Secret Lives of Children: Central questions of the course
  include, "What is the impact of race, gender, ethnicity,
  and socio-economics on developing creative identities?"
- Sound, Race, and Diaspora: "What does decolonization
  sound like, and how can we hear its resonances?"
- The Once and Future Campus poses the loaded question,
  "Can universities promote social justice, or must they
  entrench inequality?"
- Watching Sports: The class to take to "look at sports in
  the context of race, gender, and class." Olympic mixed-
  doubles ping pong will never look the same.

Serious students can still choose well, however. The Directed Studies seminars in literature and philosophy described
above can fulfill the writing requirement, as can American
Economic History; a variety of English Department survey courses on tragedies, epics, English poetry, American
literature, Shakespeare, Milton, and Chaucer; a course on
Thucydides; and Six Pretty Good Interior Journeys.

Conclusion

Were he or she determined to do so, a Yale student could easily fulfill the college's distributional requirements without receiving a genuinely liberal and general education. The Bulldog could choose the following courses (or many others), provided they are offered and available in the right order.

SOCIAL SCIENCES

- Managing Blackness in "White Space"
- American Exceptionalism

HUMANITIES AND ARTS

- Pop Sapphism
- "I Don't Like to Argue": The Styles and Politics of Humility

SCIENCE AND QUANTITATIVE REASONING

- Asian Americans and STEM
- Current Issues in Medicine and Public Health
- Approaches to International Development
- Introduction to Functions and Calculus I

WRITING AND FOREIGN LANGUAGE

- Monstrosity and the Vampire
- Watching Sports
- French

Nonetheless, a genuinely liberal and general education is possible, should a Yale student know what courses to look for. We advise, for example:

SOCIAL SCIENCES

- Directed Studies: History of Political Thought
- Classics of Justice, Morality, and the State

HUMANITIES AND ARTS

- Directed Studies: Literature
- Directed Studies: Philosophy

SCIENCE AND QUANTITATIVE REASONING

- Principles of Cell Biology
- Fundamentals of Physics
- Introductory Microeconomics
- Data Structures and Programming Techniques

WRITING AND FOREIGN LANGUAGE

- American Economic History
- Six Pretty Good Interior Journeys
- Ancient Greek

University of Pennsylvania

The general education requirements at the University of Pennsylvania vary across each of its five undergraduate programs or colleges. Here, we have focused on the requirements at Penn's School of Arts and Sciences. This curriculum has two broad objectives: to "seek to develop in [a student] some general skills or approaches to knowledge" and to "engage [a student] in the intellectual work of the disciplines in a variety of fields across the arts and sciences."

The general education requirements for the School of Arts and Sciences, therefore, are divided into Foundational Approaches and Sectors of Knowledge. Regarding the Foundational Approaches requirement, students must complete courses within six different disciplinary "approaches": Writing, Foreign Language, Formal Reasoning, Quantitative Data Analysis, Cross-Cultural Analysis, and Cultural Diversity in the US. One course is required to fulfill each distribution requirement. Through these Foundational Approaches, the college states that students "develop key intellectual capabilities demanded in a variety of disciplines."

Regarding the Sectors of Knowledge requirement,

students must finish courses within seven sectors, or subject areas: Society, History and Tradition, Arts and Letters, Humanities and Social Sciences, Living World, Physical World, and Natural Sciences Across Disciplines. One course is required to fulfill each distribution requirement. The college states that these Sectors of Knowledge allow students to "tailor their education in the arts and sciences while gaining valuable knowledge across a broad range of disciplines."

Students can choose from hundreds of courses within the general curriculum to satisfy the thirteen individual distribution requirements. While some of the courses improve students' skills in writing, formal reasoning, and diversity of languages, others appear more oriented toward entertainment, political indoctrination, or narrow specialization and do not introduce students to the most important events, ideas, and works known to humanity or ensure that students have mastered a core set of facts. It is far from clear that these courses consistently produce graduates with the advertised set of disciplinary skills.

Below, we examine the distribution requirements in Foundational Approaches and Sectors of Knowledge. Students who want a strong education can still get one, but it is easier to choose poorly and get a weak education at Penn.

Foundational Approaches

WRITING

Students can choose from about sixty writing seminars offered in 2024-25.

As at most other colleges, Penn's writing courses are often sites of activist resistance to traditional norms. This makes it simple for a student to choose a poor course. Consider these:

- Abolish the Family: This course teaches that "families can also be sites of pain, trauma, and uneven distributions of labor" and that "many people turn away from their biological families and toward 'chosen' families when in need of care, love, and understanding." Students are tasked with imagining "new models of collective care together."

- Reality TV and Gender: Students "examine the powerful cultural scripts that reality TV programming helps to create around identity, especially identities related to gender and race." Students also address questions such as, "How do these representations impact gendered and racialized bodies?" and "How does reality TV reflect, but also influence, our lived realities?"

- Questions of Normalcy: Students read Alison Kafer's *Feminist Queer Crip* and will "draw from disability studies and queer theory to consider the impacts such ideas of normalcy have on the body." The course description states, "Ultimately, we can question normalcy to understand how we are positioned as students, writers, and bodies that try to, but always exceed, being normal."

- Deliberation, Advocacy, and Civic Discourse: Students should not be misled by seeing "civic discourse" in the title. In this course, students study the rhetorical strategies involved in "coining new political vocabularies, advocating for new rights, articulating injustice, and fostering the recognition of previously unrecognized categories of identity."

- Love's Labor: The Invention of Dating: "Are you worried about your dating prospects?" Students "venture on a journey to understand how we have come to conceptualize and date the way we do."

There are also four courses related to climate change and climate activism: "Climate Emotions," "Waking Up to Climate Change," "Climate Science and Action: Earth in Crisis," and "Creating Sustainable Futures."

Is any strong course available? Preferably, Penn's writing seminars would focus on serious texts, influential thinkers, and deeply meaningful topics, to help students refine their writing skills through this engagement. Examples of great writing, in themselves, can teach. But since Penn currently offers no such seminar, the generic Writing Center course is the best available option. That's Writing Center Theory and Practice, which at least promises to advance a student's knowledge of "writing, the field of writing studies, and how to teach and learn advanced writing skills." Students also learn to refine their explanatory skills from "organizing thoughts to speaking succinctly."

FOREIGN LANGUAGE

Students have more than one hundred courses to choose from in Foreign Language this academic year. Students can choose from beginning or elementary-level classes to advanced, accelerated, or even advanced business language classes. Limited or no English is spoken in these classes.

In most courses, students are expected to develop at least a basic competence in speaking, reading, writing, and understanding a language. However, one class is limited in its teachability and student understanding of the language: Elementary Tigrinya I. In this course, students admittedly will develop "little understanding of the social conventions of conversation," and furthermore, "range and control of the language will be limited." Students are warned that "speech will largely consist of a series of short, discrete utterances."

FORMAL REASONING

For the Formal Reasoning requirement, thirty-three courses are available this academic year. These courses "focus on deductive reasoning and the formal structure of human thought, including its linguistic, logical, and mathematical constituents."

Fortunately, Penn provides several options for choosing well:

- Both Intro to Logic and Introduction to Formal Linguistics expose students to the fundamental ideas of logic, including functional logic, quantificational logic, and the formal mathematical tools for analyzing language "to understand and classify the complex structures and rules that constitute language and grammar."

- Other solid courses are Introduction to Calculus, Ideas in Mathematics, Proving Things: Algebra, Introduction to Computer Programming, and Introduction to Cognitive Science.

Courses such as these lay the groundwork for advanced study in various disciplines. They help develop critical thinking, analytical reasoning, and problem-solving skills. These skills will help students develop a balanced perspective that is resistant to the biases of current trends and ideologies. This requirement generally does a good job of prioritizing rational skills over hyper-specialized or partisan content.

A student who wants a less rigorous course could take Introduction to Theory and Musicianship. This course will "cover basic skills and vocabulary for reading, hearing, performing, analyzing, and writing music." The course is intended for non-music majors, but someone with a voice or instrumental background could probably swing through the course with ease.

QUANTITATIVE DATA ANALYSIS

In this area, students must complete a course "that uses mathematical or statistical analysis of quantitative data as an important method for understanding another subject," and students "gain experience with the use of quantitative analysis to interpret empirical data and to test hypotheses." To satisfy the requirement, about eighty-five courses are available this academic year.

Solid courses include:

- Econometric Methods and Models: Students learn "econometric techniques and their application in economic analysis and decision-making."
- Statistics for Economists: This course features "elementary probability and inferential statistical techniques."
- Quantitative Research Methods in Communication: Students will "understand the logic behind social science research, be able to view research with a critical eye, and engage in the production of research."

The following two courses, however, focus on "social justice" or activism:

- Anthropology and Praxis: Students explore trends in the public-interest applications of social science through research and evaluation. One is "problem-solving with theory and analysis in the interest of change motivated by a commitment to social justice, racial harmony, equality, and human rights."
- Explorations in Human Biology: Students are introduced to "the important contributions of biological anthropologists to the study of race, inequality, sex and gender, and health, among others."

Overall, this area is strong for having courses centered around thinking critically about quantitative data and analyses, despite the two outlier courses described above.

CROSS-CULTURAL ANALYSIS

The Cross-Cultural Analysis requirement aims to "increase students' knowledge and understanding of sociocultural systems outside the United States." More than four hundred courses can meet this requirement, suggesting that learning about any non-American culture is as worthwhile as the next.

Some of the courses are exceedingly narrow or promote group identity politics and collective guilt rather than a significant understanding of a socio-cultural system outside the United States. Some examples include:

- Decolonizing French Food: This course declares that "culinary traditions in France remain persistently rooted in legacies of colonialism that are invisible to many." To "decolonize French food," the professor will employ "the theoretical tools supplied by food studies, feminist and gender studies, critical race studies, and postcolonial studies." Avoid this course like spoiled cheese.
- Introduction to Postcolonial Literatures: Students "engage with critical perspectives on what 'post'-colonial literatures can teach us about ongoing moves to 'decolonize' universities in the Global North and beyond." That means Penn, too.
- Gender, Sexuality, and Religion: This course aims to "provide entry points into the study of religious traditions through the lens of gender." Students also "read religion through feminist and queer lenses, and they will explore the key characteristics of diverse feminist and queer studies approaches to religion, as well as limits of those approaches."
- Art, Pop, and Belonging: Or, How to Talk about Korean Popular Culture: In this very demanding course, students "look at art and talk to artists, listen to K-pop, and contemplate how these cultural representations

activate a sense of belonging and social coalition for marginalized communities in Korea." Of course, the class includes "gender and sexuality, modernity and national trauma, xenophobia and racial tensions, queer feminist movements, and cultural transnationalism in the neoliberal era."

Students looking for a worthwhile academic experience should instead choose from the following courses. The contrast between strong and weak courses in this area could hardly be clearer.

- The Decline and Fall of the Roman Empire: This course examines the Roman Empire over the span of six hundred years using "methodologies from history, archaeology, social science, and the sciences to understand the complex problem of empire and its evolutions."
- Ancient Mediterranean Empires: Students "discuss and compare ancient empires from Achaemenid Persia to Alexander the Great and the Hellenistic kingdoms of his successors to the emergence of Rome as one of the most influential empires in world history."
- World Art and Civilization Before 1400: Students first "survey the visual arts in a global context from prehistory to the dawn of the modern era." This background then serves as an introduction to the "practice of art history."

CULTURAL DIVERSITY IN THE US

Through any one of almost two hundred courses, Penn students are to "develop the skills necessary for understanding the population and culture of the United States as it becomes increasingly diverse." The university also wants students to increase their ability to "examine issues of diversity with a focus on race, ethnicity, gender, sexuality, class, and religion" through this requirement.

Unfortunately, rather than promoting unity and shared values or even a healthy pluralism, this area's emphasis on identity categories such as race, ethnicity, gender, and sexuality encourages identity politics and promotes division and conflict, as evident in the course descriptions below:

- Race, Science, and Justice: Students discuss the "significance of scientific investigations of racial difference for advancing racial justice in the United States."
- Spatial Reparations: Material and Territorial Practices of Justice: This course focuses on the "architectural, urban planning, and landscape approaches to reparations."
- Movement Song: The Poetics of Liberation: Students partake in a creative and critical poetry writing workshop that focuses on the "study of poets associated with antiwar, feminist, leftist, queer/trans, and racial justice liberatory movements."
- Introduction to Queer Art: This course exposes students to the "politics of queer art, and how and why in the US, even amidst often dangerous homophobia, it was queer artists who represented America to itself."
- Introduction to Sexuality Studies and Queer Theory: Students learn about "queer theory's conceptual heritage and prehistory in psychoanalysis, deconstruction, and poststructuralism, the history of sexuality, gay and lesbian studies, woman-of-color feminism, the feminist sex wars, and the AIDS crisis."
- Topics of Psychology in Education: Psychoeducational Processes with Black Males: The core tenets of this course convey that "racial oppression exists, matters, is ubiquitous and pernicious and that those most affected are ignorant of this reality." Students learn "how to help Black boys and men they engage in identifying and challenging the effects of racial oppression on their academic, occupational, relational, and cultural well-being, and to promote post-traumatic growth."

Penn offers very few classes that avoid divisive, hyper-specialized content or that fail to privilege certain identity groups. These two courses, though, enable students to do better:

- Law and Society: This course introduces students to the "major theoretical concepts concerning law and society," with class discussions centering around "civil liberties, the organization of courts, legislatures, the legal profession, and administrative agencies."
- The American West: Students learn about the "vast and varied region now known as the American West, and the earlier 'wests' that preceded it."

Overall, Penn students would be better off without the "cultural diversity" requirement at all.

Sectors of Knowledge

SOCIETY

The primary objective of Society courses is to "enable students to develop concepts and principles, test theories, and perfect tools that can be used to interpret, explain, and evaluate the behavior of human beings in contemporary societies." Nearly sixty courses are available this year.

Choosing poorly means taking a course focused on social structures, identities, or climate change:

- Sociology of Race and Ethnicity: Students explore "racial and ethnic identity, assimilation of immigrants, immigrants' legal status, forms of racism and bias, white privilege, and intersectionality." Students also examine policies that have "perpetuated racial and ethnic inequality as well as those that attempt to ameliorate it."

- Sociology of Gender: Students learn how gender "is an organizing principle of society, shaping social structures, cultural understandings, processes of interaction, and identities in ways that have profound consequences." They will also be taught "how gender is socially constructed and how structural constraints limit choice."
- The Family: Students examine how families are organized "along the lines of gender, sexuality, social class, and race and how this affects family life." Students also explore the topic of how "family life is continuously changing while, at the same time, traditional gender roles persist" and how "greedy workplaces" are creating "work-family conflicts for mothers and fathers." Additionally, students are to examine "diverse family forms," such as families "headed by same-gender parents and families headed by gender non-conforming parents."
- Nature, Culture, Environmentalism: This course exposes students to some of the "emergent debates in the fields of climate studies and environmental justice" and discusses possible tools to "think, mitigate, and adapt to the effects of climate change."

Choosing well means focusing on economics or other courses that are foundational to understanding American society:

- Introduction to Microeconomics: Students are introduced to "economic analysis and its application" along with the "theory of supply and demand, costs and revenues of the firm under perfect competition, pricing of factors of production, income distribution, and theory of international trade."
- Introduction to American Politics: This course teaches students the "basics of American politics and government" while reviewing the "historical and philosophical foundations of the American Republic."

- Introduction to Comparative Politics: This course introduces students to "comparative political analysis." Students use core concepts and theories to analyze "the political behavior, circumstances, institutions, and dynamic patterns of change that people experience in very different societies."

HISTORY AND TRADITION

To meet the History and Tradition requirement, students must take one of about one hundred courses that are expected to teach them "to interpret primary sources, identify and discuss their core intellectual issues, understand the social contexts in which these sources were created, pose questions about their validity and ability to represent broader perspectives, and utilize them when writing persuasive essays."

As a distribution requirement, this area functions well, judging from course descriptions. Unfortunately, Penn has no requirement to learn American history or the history of Western civilization. There are not even many choices for students who wish to do so. Even the "Deciphering America" class, described below, only focuses on a few "telling moments in history." Absent reform, History and Tradition will continue to be a missed opportunity—another vague distribution requirement.

The several best bets in this area are:

- Introduction to the Ancient Middle East: A course on the "history, society, and culture of the ancient Middle East, in particular, Egypt and Mesopotamia," where students review many "ancient texts in translation," including the *Epic of Gilgamesh*, and "various archaeological and art historical materials."
- Great Transformations: This course "explores the history and archaeology of the last twenty thousand years

from the development of agriculture to the Industrial Revolution."

- Ancient Mediterranean Empires: This course teaches students to "discuss and compare ancient empires from Achaemenid Persia to Alexander the Great and the Hellenistic kingdoms of his successors to the emergence of Rome as one of the most influential empires in world history."

- Ancient Greek Philosophy: This course helps students "trace the origins of philosophy as a discipline in the Western tradition, looking to the thinkers of Ancient Greece and Rome."

- Origins of Nazism: From Democracy to Race War and Genocide: Students learn first about "Germany's first democracy, the Weimar Republic and its vibrant political culture" and then about the "Nazi regime and how it consolidated its power and remade society based on the concepts of race and struggle."

- First-Year Seminar: Reading the Classics: This course examines the "early roots of Western culture—the Biblical, Greek, and Roman traditions—as well as how sixteenth- and seventeenth-century Europeans reproduced, rethought, and reshaped these early traditions."

- Deciphering America: This course "examines American history from the first contacts of the indigenous peoples of North America with European settlers to our times by focusing on several telling moments in this history." Students are exposed to "specific primary document(s), historical figure(s), image(s), or cultural artifact(s)" to understand each topic better.

If a Penn student still wants an oppression narrative, there are a few choices. The most interesting and anti-Western among them may be Getting Crusaded, covering two hundred years "from the perspective of the invaded, rather than the invaders."

ARTS AND LETTERS

Penn's objective for Arts and Letters courses is to "confront students with works of creativity; cultivate their powers of perception (visual, textual, auditory); and equip them with tools for analysis, interpretation, and criticism." About 175 courses can meet the requirement this academic year.

Here are some of the most worthwhile Arts and Letters courses:

- Ancient Drama: This course introduces students to "some of the greatest works for dramatic literature in the Western canon." Students consider the "social, political, religious, and artistic functions of drama in ancient Greece and Rome and discuss both differences and similarities between ancient drama and modern art forms."
- National Epics: Students "consider texts that become 'national epics,' texts that in some sense come to 'represent' a nation."
- 1000 Years of Musical Listening: This course explores the "technical workings of music and the vocabularies for analyzing music and articulating a response to it."
- Introduction to Modern South Asian Literatures: This course presents "a wide-ranging introduction to the literatures of South Asia from roughly 1500 to the present, as well as an exploration of their histories and impact on South Asian society today."
- World Film History to 1945: Students "develop methods for analyzing film while examining the growth of film as an art, an industry, a technology, and a political instrument."

Some courses that are least worth taking include:

- Monsters in Film and Literature: This course "studies literature and film featuring a wide assortment of monsters

across a range of genres, cultures, and time periods." This
course also inevitably includes readings in "race, gender,
and cultural studies and literary theory."

- Sex and Representation: Students "explore literature that
  resists normative categories of gender and sexuality."
  They are taught how "non-normative desire is produced
  and policed by social and literary contexts—and how
  those contexts can be re-imagined and transformed."

- Decolonizing French Food: This course, mentioned
  above, is also a stinky option to fulfill the Arts and Letters distribution requirement.

HUMANITIES AND SOCIAL SCIENCES

Penn's Humanities and Social Sciences distribution requirement is extremely vague. The point is merely to
broaden students' perspective of the humanities and
social sciences "by taking a course that also cuts across
the previous sectors of Society, History and Tradition,
and Arts and Letters." Any of about seventy-five courses
will count.

Good options are available. These include:

- Cold War: Global History: Students "examine the Cold
  War as a global phenomenon, covering not only the
  military and diplomatic history of the period but also examining the social and cultural impact of the superpower
  confrontation."

- Introduction to Philosophy: This course introduces
  some of the difficult questions philosophers ask about
  the "most basic issues in human life" and the "methods philosophers have developed for thinking clearly
  about them."

- Law and Literature: Students receive an introduction
  "not only to the representations of the law and legal
  processes in literary texts, but also to the theories of

reading, representation, and interpretation that form the foundation of both legal and literary analysis."

Choosing poorly is easy—just select one of these:

- Design, Race, and Climate Justice: Using a critical and historical lens, students "will examine material, spatial, and ecological practices in architecture and design that perpetuate racial inequities and exacerbate climate injustices."
- Introduction to Acting: This course takes students "step by step through the practical work an actor must do to live and behave truthfully on stage." Students partake in "relaxation and physical exercise, interactive games, ensemble building, etc."
- Virtual Reality Storytelling: Students "prototype their own VR narrative films" while also using the "critical theory of media scholars from diverse backgrounds to critique VR applications as models to inform their iterative design process."
- Gender, Sexuality, and Religion: This course shows how gender is "taught, performed, and regulated" and its relation to religion. Students also explore the "key characteristics of diverse feminist and queer studies approaches to religion."

LIVING WORLD

The Living World area "deals substantively with the evolution, development, structure, and function of living systems." Students must complete one course among about twenty-three options.

The courses listed are, for the most part, standard science courses that are closely related to the science of living organisms. For example:

- Introduction to Biology A: This course teaches the "basic chemistry of life, cell biology, molecular biology, and genetics in all living organisms."

- Introduction to Biology B: "Evolution, physiology, development, and ecology in all living organisms."
- Introduction to Brain and Behavior: An "introduction to the structure and function of the vertebrate nervous system."

Courses that are less directly related to the study of living organisms and their functions are also options:

- Neuroscience and Society: Students "examine how neuroscience is being applied in law, criminal justice, national defense, education, economics, business, and other sectors of society." This course seems long on "society" and relatively short on neuroscience.
- Introduction to Experimental Psychology: This course provides an "introduction to the basic topics of psychology, including our three major areas of distribution: the biological basis of behavior, the cognitive basis of behavior, and individual and group bases of behavior." Good in itself but not well related to the requirement.
- Forensic Neuroscience: This course helps students "understand and interpret the use of behavioral neuro evidence in the justice system."

PHYSICAL WORLD

For this distribution requirement, students are expected to gain insight into the "content and workings of modern physical science." The courses meeting this requirement generally rise to the challenge. While some courses require a mathematics prerequisite, lighter courses explore the "historical development of a subject" and "its conceptual notions and their mathematical expressions." This year, there are about twenty courses to choose from.

Typical courses offered include:

- General Chemistry I: Students are taught the "basic concepts and principles of chemistry and their applications in chemistry and closely related fields."

- General Chemistry II: This course includes topics related to the "thermodynamic approach to chemical reactions, electrochemical processes, and reaction rates and mechanisms."
- Earth Systems Science: This course teaches about Earth as a complex system "through [an] examination of its atmosphere, hydrosphere, lithosphere, and biosphere, the interactions among these spheres, and of the human impacts on the planet and its responses."
- General Physics: Mechanics, Heat, and Sound: This course includes an "introduction to the classical laws of motion, including kinematics, forces in nature, Newton's laws of motions, conservation of energy and momentum, fluid statics and dynamics, oscillations, and waves."
- Introduction to Astrophysics I: Students learn about "Newtonian gravity and the properties of light and matter as they are relevant for understanding astrophysical objects."

One oddball class, however, is The Phonetics of Music. In this course, students are introduced to the "methods for quantifying aspects of voice production" and the "scientific basis for some vocal techniques."

NATURAL SCIENCES ACROSS DISCIPLINES

In this area, students "engage with diverse perspectives generated by applying the principles of the natural sciences to broader applications." Almost sixty courses count this year.

Most courses in this area look academically challenging and worthwhile. Some of these are:

- Theoretical and Computational Neuroscience: This course will "develop theoretical and computational approaches to structural and functional organization in the brain."

- Introduction to Computational Physics: Students become familiar with "computational tools utilized to solve common problems that arise in physics."
- Foundations of Data Science: This course covers a range of topics: "basic programming, data manipulation, data visualization, randomness, probability, statistics, predictions, interpreting results, and data ethics."
- Structural Biology: How "biological properties are determined by the microscopic chemical properties of proteins and biomacromolecules."

For students wanting an easier exploration, a less rigorous course that is intended for majors outside of the physical sciences and engineering is The Solar System, Exoplanets, and Life. This is a survey course on "planets and life covering our solar system and exoplanets orbiting other stars."

Meanwhile, for those more interested in activism and less in science itself, there is Repairing the Planet: Tools for the Climate Emergency. This course, which takes "the climate emergency" for granted, is a "comprehensive introduction to the climate emergency and the tools with which we can fight it."

Penn Students Can Choose Distribution Courses Wisely or Poorly

The general education requirements at the University of Pennsylvania aim to provide a well-rounded and academically rigorous education. However, while some courses meet this standard, many others fall short, leading to a fragmented and incomplete educational experience, often advancing activism instead of scholarship. As a result, outside of the sciences, Penn's undergraduate education functions more as marshmallow distribution requirements than as a true core curriculum that guarantees a strong, consistent academic foundation for all students.

Below, we present two paths that students can take to fulfill all general education requirements at the University of Pennsylvania. A student who wants to coast academically and crusade for social justice can get away with the first option, while the second option shows how dedicated Penn students could receive a real education.

The Weak Option

WRITING AND FOREIGN LANGUAGE

- Reality TV and Gender
- Elementary Tigrinya I

FORMAL REASONING AND QUANTITATIVE DATA ANALYSIS

- Introduction to Theory and Musicianship
- Explorations in Human Biology

CROSS-CULTURAL ANALYSIS AND CULTURAL DIVERSITY IN THE US

- Decolonizing French Food
- Introduction to Queer Art

SOCIETY

- Sociology of Race and Ethnicity

HISTORY AND TRADITION

- Getting Crusaded

ARTS AND LETTERS

- Monsters in Film and Literature

HUMANITIES AND SOCIAL SCIENCES

- Virtual Reality Storytelling

"HARD" SCIENCES

- Introduction to Experimental Psychology
- The Phonetics of Music
- Repairing the Planet: Tools for the Climate Emergency

The Strong Option

WRITING AND FOREIGN LANGUAGE

- Writing Center Theory and Practice
- Elementary Classical Greek I

FORMAL REASONING AND QUANTITATIVE DATA ANALYSIS

- Intro to Logic
- Econometric Methods and Models

CROSS-CULTURAL ANALYSIS AND CULTURAL DIVERSITY IN THE US

- Ancient Mediterranean Empires
- Law and Society

SOCIETY

- Introduction to Microeconomics

HISTORY AND TRADITION

- First-Year Seminar: Reading the Classics

ARTS AND LETTERS

- Ancient Drama

HUMANITIES AND SOCIAL SCIENCES

- Introduction to Philosophy

HARD SCIENCES

- Introduction to Biology A
- General Physics: Mechanics, Heat, and Sound
- Foundations of Data Science

Harvard University

To fulfill their general education requirements, Harvard College undergraduates must complete four general education courses, one from each of the following four categories: Aesthetics and Culture; Ethics and Civics; Histories, Societies, Individuals; and Science and Technology in Society.

In addition, undergraduates must complete the college's language, expository writing, distribution, and "quantitative reasoning with data" requirements. Combined with the general education courses above, these courses constitute the Harvard College core curriculum. To receive a bachelor's degree, students also must complete a major or "concentration" and enough electives to have a total of 128 credits (two-thirds of which must have grades of C– or better).

In brief, Harvard intends its core requirements to involve the following preparation:

- **General Education**: A "broad foundation that enables students to make meaningful connections across disciplines" and to connect the subjects students study to the people and the world that they will experience beyond the classroom. These courses function as distribution requirements—any one course in each of four categories will count.

- **Divisional Distribution**: Students will experience the "diversity of scholarly disciplines at Harvard."
- **Quantitative Reasoning with Data**: Courses introduce "mathematical, statistical, and computational methods" that will equip students to analyze data critically within various disciplines.
- **Expository Writing**: First-year students are taught "the fundamentals of academic writing," which includes "analytic composition and revision."
- **Language**: Completing the language requirement will "allow a student to develop a firsthand understanding of linguistic and cultural variety" and prepare students to "thrive in international and multilingual contexts and become leaders of change in a globalized workplace."

When a college like Harvard requires no particular content in its core curriculum—forgoing a series of required courses in the arts and sciences in favor of broad distribution requirements with many options but no required content—it risks leaving students with a fragmented and incomplete education. Harvard's distributional approach offers no assurance that students will acquire any set of fundamental facts appropriate to becoming an educated, successful adult.

It's possible for undergraduates to find courses that help them to become informed and productive citizens and lifelong learners. However, slackers who stack exclusively niche courses will end up with narrow and distorted views of themselves, other individuals and groups, American society and its history, and the rest of the world. "It was all shock and bewilderment on Harvard's campus today," one member of Harvard's Class of 2025 wrote, as students learned that more than half of the country's voters chose a Republican for president. Inconceivable!

Harvard University

General Education

AESTHETICS AND CULTURE

Harvard's Aesthetics and Culture courses purportedly "foster critical engagement with diverse artistic and creative endeavors and traditions across history and geographical locations, helping students situate themselves and others as participants in and products of art and culture." In the Fall 2024 and Spring 2025 semesters, they may choose from among eighteen options.

Choosing poorly means selecting one of the following niche or politicized courses:

- Power to the People: Black Power, Radical Feminism, and Gay Liberation: Students ask, "How does understanding political activists and movements in the past help us radically change the world today?"
- Stories from the End of the World: Students contemplate why "imagining the end is so pervasive in contemporary cultures," but "most of the work will be focused on contemporary cultural products, such as movies, short stories, songs, art, comic books, videogames, and so on." Apparently, for their final project, students "reflect about your own fantasy of the end and write (or photograph, or sing) it."
- *Anime* as Global Popular Culture: Students learn to engage with "Japanese or Japanese-style animation through evaluating the aesthetic and socio-cultural relevance of *anime* and also the cultural value of *anime*."
- Eating Culture: Past, Present, and Future: This course is dedicated to exploring "the act of eating, in human civilization from ancient to contemporary, and all the processes associated with eating—including finding, making, enjoying, and talking about food, etc."

Choosing well means selecting one of the following:

- Faith and Authenticity: Religion, Existentialism, and the Human Condition: This course introduces students to "central questions in Western philosophy of religion through close reading of fundamental texts in existentialism with attention to selected philosophical and theological sources." The course focuses on the following themes: "authenticity and absurdity, finitude and death, faith and ambiguity, and the quest for freedom and responsibility."
- The Ancient Greek Hero: This course asks students, "How did ancient Greek heroes, both male and female, learn about life by facing what all of us have to face, our human condition?" Students reflect on the "meaning of life and death in the light of what they read in Greek literature about the ordeals of becoming a hero."
- What is a Book? From the Clay Tablet to the Kindle: Students study "the many different material forms in which texts in Western culture have been inscribed—from tablets to e-books—and the technologies that have enabled their creation." The books "will range from the Bible to Vesalius, from Homer to *Harold and His Purple Crayon*. Sections will visit the Weissman Preservation Center, Houghton Library, Fine Arts Special Collections, and the Harvard Art Museum, and all students are required to study a manuscript close-up and participate in a printing workshop."

ETHICS AND CIVICS

In the Ethics and Civics category, courses "examine the dilemmas that individuals, communities, and societies face as they explore the questions of virtue, justice, equity, inclusion, and the greater good." Fourteen courses in 2024–25 meet the requirement.

The worst of the bunch is Ethics of Climate Change, which takes the science for granted and skips ahead to the ethics: "What are individuals, scientists, businesses, and governments morally required to do to prevent catastrophic climate change?"

The best choice is What is a Republic? In this course, students "consider systems of governance in Republican Rome, medieval Europe, early modern England and France, Native American nations, and the United States." As the course description puts it, "The thinkers and founders you will read thought long and hard [about] what freedom is, how to balance executive and legislative power, and why republics and democracies can be unstable."

Another valuable course, Reclaiming Argument: Logic as a Force for Good, was offered in Spring 2024 but unfortunately is not offered in 2024–25. In this course, students learned how argumentation can be reclaimed for a more noble purpose: "to build genuine understanding between people, even across profound differences of viewpoint." Considering that Harvard's climate for free speech is consistently classified as "abysmal" by the Foundation for Individual Rights and Expression (FIRE), more such courses would improve Harvard's oppressive culture. (FIRE has noted that over the past few years, Harvard has sanctioned scholars, revoked a student's acceptance over comments made on social media, disinvited speakers based on political views, and allowed students to shout down invited campus speakers.)

In 2024, Harvard anti-Israel protestors hoisted a Palestinian flag in place of the US flag, following days of a pro-Palestine encampment taking over part of the campus. Later, the university and its leadership announced in May 2024 that the institution would "refrain from taking official positions on controversial public policy issues." Harvard's curriculum ought to follow such an academic rather than activist approach.

In the meantime, courses on civil discourse would benefit everyone, regardless of background or discipline, by helping foster understanding and bridging profound differences of viewpoint.

HISTORIES, SOCIETIES, INDIVIDUALS

In the current academic year, seventeen courses are offered to students in the History, Societies, Individuals category. These courses "explore the dynamic relationships between individuals and larger social, economic, and political structures, historically and in the present moment."

Students should choose better courses than these:

- Guns in the US: A Love Story: For this course, students quickly realize it's a hate story: "Why does America love guns? . . . How did the nation become a 'gun culture,' and whose rights and interests does widespread armament serve?"
- Mexico and the Making of Global Cuisine: Students "investigate how, when, where, and why various changes in Mexican cuisine took place." It's interesting but too narrow for a core course.
- Moctezuma's Mexico Then and Now: Ancient Empires, Race Mixture, and Finding Latinx: "The emphasis is on the mythical and social origins, glory days, and political collapse of the Aztec Empire and Maya civilizations as a pivot to the study of the sexual, religious, and racial interactions of the Great Encounter between Mesoamerica, Africa, Europe, and the independent nations of Mexico and the United States." Human sacrifice in these empires goes unmentioned in the course description.

Many of the available courses are like these—hostile to American civilization, narrow, or unlikely to represent diverse viewpoints. Dishonorable mention goes to a course last taught in 2023, Race in a Polarized America, which wondered, if "the US at its core [is] a white supremacist society." Accordingly, good options are limited. The course What Is a Republic? mentioned above counts for this area's requirement. A student also should consider one of these:

- Deep History: Students explore human history and tens of thousands of years of human existence via archaeology and related disciplines. They will also review material remains and the collection of historical artifacts at Harvard's various museums.
- Power and Civilization: China: In short, this wide-ranging course "explores how the world's largest and oldest bureaucratic state has dealt with enduring problems of economic and political organization."

SCIENCE AND TECHNOLOGY IN SOCIETY

Science and Technology courses "explore scientific and technological ideas and practices in their social and historical contexts, providing a foundation to assess their promise and perils." Twenty-four courses are available in 2024–25.

Very few of these courses promise to integrate substantial study of the hard sciences, such as physics, chemistry, or biology. Classes include sleep, human nature, cooking, climate change, and so on. Although they surely include some science, the evidence suggests a *Scientific American* level of sophistication in most courses. Indeed, these courses mainly focus on "society" and lack rigorous learning of scientific or technological principles.

Choosing most poorly would mean selecting one of these:

- Science and Cooking: Students "watch as chefs reveal secrets behind some of their most famous culinary recipes."

- Human Nature: This course includes the "evolutionary origins of human behavior [and how that informs contemporary issues] such as homosexuality, racism, and the use of oral contraceptives."
- Psychotherapy and the Modern Self: "The conflicts and controversies that characterize today's psychotherapeutic landscape, addressing questions concerning its present condition and prospects." It's interesting material, but the course promises little science. Instead, it offers to "examine therapy's long-overdue, ongoing reckoning with racial issues, gendered identities, and access to treatment."

Furthermore, four of the courses in this area are specifically about climate change, likely reflecting Harvard's non-neutral climate commitment:

- Human Evolution, Climate Change, and Health
- Confronting Climate Change: A Foundation in Science, Technology, and Policy
- The Challenge of Human-Induced Climate Change: Transitioning to a Post–Fossil Fuel Future
- Climate Crossroads

The best option here is Great Experiments that Changed Our World. In this course, students "carry out the same investigations [as in ten classic experiments], building [their] own simple equipment from scratch, duplicating the challenges of wresting patterns from noisy and incomplete data." They will also "build an understanding of the nature of scientific progress, examining how the mastery of natural phenomena leads to new technologies and how these can contribute to further scientific discovery."

LANGUAGE

For the language requirement, students must take one year-long or two semester-long courses or submit test scores demonstrating a certain level of proficiency. Harvard affirms "that learning a language other than English is an essential component of a liberal arts and science education and that this learning should allow a student to develop first-hand understanding of linguistic and cultural variety." Harvard offers German, Japanese, Italian, Swedish, Spanish, and many more language courses. Students are not allowed to count foreign literature courses conducted in English to meet the language requirement.

EXPOSITORY WRITING

Undergraduates must take one or two courses in expository writing in their first year, depending on their skill level as determined by a writing exam. Students who need to take a year of "Expos" begin with Expos 10; others enroll directly in a more advanced writing class on a specific topic, Expos 20. For the advanced writing class, students have close to thirty courses available for the fall term.

Writing courses at Harvard, as elsewhere, tend to make cultural critique the basis for developing skills in academic writing. Here are the worst offenders:

- Breaking the Norm: Students explore questions such as, "Does acceptance into mainstream social institutions like marriage come at the cost of more radical change and the celebration of true difference?" and "Do standard ways of looking in visual media and film perpetuate the sexual objectification of women?" Students also read short literary works from first-wave feminists and hear from queer theorists on different films from the 2000s. One of the class's objectives is to "learn to defamiliarize the normal, making it suddenly strange in the process" and to expose "the normal as mere prevalence or habit."
- Gender and Mental Health: Students learn about the "constructs of gender and mental health" and "how

gender leads to illness." They also read and evaluate competing theories "about the relative import of biological sex differences; gender norms and socialization; gender-based inequities, stressors, and trauma; and over-pathologizing women and gender-expansive individuals." Students also explore "what history can teach us about conducting clinical science in a patriarchal but post-binary world."

- More Than a Game: This course treats "the complex relationship of race to American sports culture and the political dynamics of consequential events within the sporting world." Students also consider the following questions: "What makes the world of sports such a significant setting for political activism? What authority lies in the manipulation of athletic culture by politicians?" and much more along these lines.

- Queer Coming of Age Stories: Students "analyze queer coming of age stories in literature, film, and popular culture." Students think about how traditional "coming of age stories" have excluded "queer youth" and how including them changes how such stories are told. Students also examine films related to "coming out stories" and "heteronormativity" and will ultimately be charged with making a "researched argument about a queer coming of age story of their own choosing."

- Thinking with Conspiracies: This course examines "the history and inner logic of conspiracy theories." It mentions "QAnon," "Rigged elections," and "Anti-Vaxxers" as the conspiracy theories of today.

We have nothing to strongly recommend for Expos 20. Harvard should take a closer look at decision-making in Expos to create a more intellectually serious writing program. Since a serious student must take *something*, we suggest Free Speech in a Digital World. Note, however, that the course's ethos is against free speech. A proponent of free expression will need to grapple with the many exceptions to free speech that the course proposes. Another possibility is What Does It Mean to Win? Fairness, Value, and Negotiation, which will "consider negotiation tactics and concepts about fairness," including both philosophical and practical considerations.

Divisional Distribution Requirements

Beyond the distribution requirements described above, students must complete one departmental course in each of the three main divisions of the Faculty of Arts and Sciences and the Paulson School of Engineering and Applied Sciences: Arts and Humanities, Social Sciences, and Science and Engineering and Applied Science. The distribution requirement purportedly "exposes students to the diversity of scholarly disciplines." The wide breadth of the options, however, means that the quality of students' academic experiences can diverge widely.

ARTS AND HUMANITIES

In 2024–25, about 450 courses meet the Arts and Humanities divisional requirement. Plenty of courses are poor choices for students, and these are some of the worst offenders:

- *The Exorcist*: Trigger warning! "Briefly America's most terrifying movie, now an inexhaustible source of camp, reference, and technique, William Friedkin's *The Exorcist* is a rich allegory of postwar America. . . . The book and film contain offensive language, depictions of sexual and domestic violence, sacrilegious treatment of religious icons, realistically depicted invasive medical procedures, and expulsion of bodily fluids. We will be treating these subjects with care."

- Global Transgender Histories: Students will "understand the impacts of phenomena such as racism, imperialism, and medicalization on gender identities, particularly since the nineteenth century."
- Zombies, Witchcraft, and Uncanny Science: Students explore "scientific advancements that push the boundaries of what is considered normal and rational through topics such as genetic engineering, artificial intelligence, and transhumanism."
- Queer Archives: Students read about "dissident voices representing gender and sexual subjectivities while also cultivating a practice of reading against the grain as a way of attending to the exclusionary operations of representational practices."

A student disposed toward academic objectivity or historical rigor might instead take one of the following:

- Introduction to the Ancient Greek World: The "history of ancient Greece from the Bronze Age Minoan and Mycenaean palace civilizations to the Roman conquest of the East Mediterranean." Students also explore a wide variety of written records and archaeological findings that historians use to comprehend ancient Greece.
- Introduction to Ancient Greek and Roman Philosophy: An "introduction to some of the most influential theories in Ancient Greek and Roman Philosophy."

SCIENCE AND ENGINEERING

About 270 courses meet this requirement in this academic year. Most, if not all, appear to teach the hard sciences or engage in similarly rigorous topics.

Offerings include:

- Introduction to Applied Mathematics: "An introduction to the problems and issues of applied mathematics, focusing on areas where mathematical ideas have had a major impact on diverse fields of human inquiry."

- Physics as a Foundation for Science and Engineering: The "first half of a year-long, team- and project-based introduction to physics focusing on the application of physics to real-world problems."
- Principles of Organic Chemistry: An "introduction to organic chemistry, with an emphasis on structure and bonding, reaction mechanisms, and chemical reactivity."
- Statistical Thermodynamics: An "introduction to statistical mechanics, thermodynamics, and chemical kinetics with applications to problems in chemistry and biology."
- Computational Thinking and Problem-Solving: An "introduction to computational thinking, useful concepts in the field of computer science, and the art of computer programming using Python."

An outlier course, however, is "Global Wetlands: Boundary-spanning Ecosystems for Science, Social Justice, and Public Policy." The course description says that wetlands are "crucial components of climate change resilience and adaptation policies" and "serve as sites of social justice and cultural heritage."

SOCIAL SCIENCES

More than seven hundred courses are available to students to fulfill the Social Sciences distribution requirement.

Choosing poorly is simple, and here are some of the worst:

- Ethnic Studies and Education: Students explore topics such as "settler colonialism, oppression, intergenerational trauma, white supremacy, solidarity, social change," and much more.
- Harvard and Native Lands: Students are told that "Harvard's endowment included Native lands expropriated through war, theft, and coercion."

- Political Violence in the Twentieth Century: This course equates January 6th rioters with school shooters. Students are challenged to "think historically (and hence critically) about the ways in which violence functions in contemporary politics."
- Climate Responsibility and Climate Action: Students address, "Who bears responsibility for climate change?" The course description states, "Confronting this question is central to establishing equitable policies to reduce greenhouse gas emissions and limit the adverse impacts of now unavoidable climate disruption."
- #AbolishPolice: The Politics of Public Safety in the Age of Social Media: Here, students "analyze and interrogate topics relating to institutional justice, systemic inequality and racism, abolitionist thought, social movements, and internet culture." This class requires students to listen to a podcast discussing Ibram X. Kendi's book *How to Be an Antiracist*, selections from the *New York Times'* "1619 Project," and much more.
- The Means of Reproduction: Health, Bodies, Technologies: Students situate the "use of [reproductive] technologies in relation to racialized histories of colonialism, feminist movements, Cold War conflicts, postcolonial stat-making, and contemporary right-wing nationalists."
- Legitimacy and Resistance in an Unjust World: This course declares that "there is, after all, a great deal of injustice, violence, suffering, and violation of freedom in our world, both inflicted upon each other and as inaction on climate change foretells upon generations to come." Students analyze "conceptions of justice and legitimacy and consider justifications for various forms of unlawful dissent, from civil disobedience to militant resistance to revolution, when political institutions fail to govern justly or legitimately."

- Fascism and Far-Right Movements: This course asks students to contemplate the question, "What is 'new' or 'alternative' about contemporary far-right movements, and what are their connections, if any, to fascist (or colonial) legacies of the past?"
- Inequality Under Capitalism: This course states that "All capitalist societies are characterized by significant forms of inequality." Students ponder, "Why do some people have more than others? Second, what should be done about these facts? What does justice require?"

Meanwhile, a student who wants to avoid partisanship or bias or is seeking an objective exploration of a specific subject or topic may opt to take one of the following:

- Comparative Political Development: The main objective of this course is for students to "understand how the roots of political development in different countries connect with their politics and economies today."
- Western Intellectual History: The Prehistory of Modern Thought: This course is a "survey of major themes in medieval and early modern intellectual history." Readings will include the writings of "Anselm, Abelard, Thomas Aquinas, William of Ockham, Petrarch, Machiavelli, Thomas More, Martin Luther, Montaigne, Francis Bacon, Descartes, and Hobbes."

QUANTITATIVE REASONING WITH DATA

Students must take one course to satisfy this general education requirement, which "introduces students to mathematical, statistical, and computational methods that will enable students to think critically about data." Most, though not all, of the seventy-six courses from which to choose are rigorous and academically challenging. Some of these are:

- Data Science 1: Introduction to Data Science: The course treats "the analysis of messy, real-life data to perform predictions using statistical and machine learning methods."
- Introduction to Econometrics: An "introduction to multiple regression techniques with a focus on economic applications."
- Quantitative Methods in Economics: This course includes "conditional expectations and its linear approximation; best linear predictors; omitted variable bias; panel data methods and the role of unobserved heterogeneity; instrumental variables and the role of randomization; [and] various approaches to inference on causal relations."
- Introduction to Computer Science: This course "teaches you how to solve problems, both with and without code, with an emphasis on correctness, design, and style. Topics generally include computational thinking, abstraction, algorithms, data structures, and computer science."

A few courses, however, are less academically challenging and not worthwhile compared with the others:

- Data Analysis and Politics: This course asks, "How can we measure racial discrimination in job hiring?"
- Celestial Navigation: This course helps students gain "expertise in using navigators' tools (sextant, compass, and charts) while learning the steps to the celestial dance of the sun, moon, stars, and planets." This course ends with a "day-long cruise to practice navigation skills." Fun, perhaps, but relatively insubstantial.
- Using Big Data to Solve Economic and Social Problems with Laboratory Component: The methods part of the course may be valuable, but too much of the course merely includes "discussions with leading researchers and practitioners who use big data in real-world applications. Topics include equality of opportunity, education, racial

disparities, innovation and entrepreneurship, health care, climate change, criminal justice, tax policy, and poverty in developing countries."

- Sounds of Language: This class "introduces students to the sounds of the world's languages and provides tools for studying them systematically."

Conclusion: Harvard's Distribution Requirements Are Generally Weak

The General Education requirements at Harvard are dressed-up distribution requirements like those at most other Ivy League universities. The many course offerings to meet each requirement encompass a broad spectrum of topics, leading to vastly different educational experiences based on individual student choices. And judging by course descriptions, those experiences also can be either rigorous or, much more likely, weak and politicized.

This is not to argue that no strong options are available. Students can still choose their courses well. But the presence of so many less worthwhile courses risks leaving students with a fragmented, incomplete, and biased education.

If Harvard were committed to fostering truly interdisciplinary learning, its faculty would do the hard work of identifying a more limited range of valuable content, not shirking this duty by claiming, for instance, that having completed any social science course from a huge list is sufficient for a graduate to count as a Harvard-educated adult.

Harvard's distribution requirements do not prepare students to become informed citizens, effective workers, lifelong learners, or distinguished leaders. A student must carefully sift the wheat from the chaff. But an undergraduate can hardly be expected to have the intellectual preparation needed to take a critical eye to Harvard's own proffered curriculum.

To help students who want a rigorous Harvard education and to illustrate the opposite, we present here two paths students can take to fulfill Harvard College's requirements at the university.

A Weak Path

EXPOSITORY WRITING

- Queer Coming-of-Age Stories

AESTHETICS AND CULTURE

- Anime as Global Popular Culture

ETHICS AND CIVICS

- Ethics of Climate Change

HISTORIES, SOCIETIES, AND INDIVIDUALS

- Guns in the US: A Love Story

SCIENCE AND TECHNOLOGY IN SOCIETY

- Psychotherapy and the Modern Self

QUANTITATIVE REASONING WITH DATA

- Celestial Navigation

LANGUAGE

- Beginning French I: Cross-Cultural Encounters in French; Beginning French II

DIVISIONAL DISTRIBUTION

- *Arts and Humanities*: Zombies, Witchcraft, and Uncanny Science
- *Social Sciences*: Ethnic Studies and Education
- *Science and Engineering*: Global Wetlands: Boundary-spanning Ecosystems for Science, Social Justice, and Public Policy

A Strong Path

EXPOSITORY WRITING

- Free Speech in a Digital World (but no course is truly satisfactory)

AESTHETICS AND CULTURE

- Faith and Authenticity: Religion, Existentialism, and the Human Condition

ETHICS AND CIVICS

- What is a Republic?

HISTORIES, SOCIETIES, AND INDIVIDUALS

- Deep History

SCIENCE AND TECHNOLOGY IN SOCIETY

- Great Experiments that Changed Our World

QUANTITATIVE REASONING WITH DATA

- Quantitative Methods in Economics

LANGUAGE

- Introductory Ancient Greek 1 and 2

DIVISIONAL DISTRIBUTION

- *Arts and Humanities*: Introduction to Ancient Greek and Roman Philosophy
- *Social Sciences*: Western Intellectual History: The Prehistory of Modern Thought
- *Science and Engineering*: Physics as a Foundation for Science and Engineering

PRINCETON
UNIVERSITY

P rinceton University's general education requirements differ between its two undergraduate de-
grees, the Bachelor of Arts (A.B.) and the Bachelor
of Science in Engineering (B.S.E.). Here we focus on the
A.B. requirements, since the A.B. is the more common
undergraduate degree.

For Princeton, A.B. students must complete ten distribution requirements. Six require one course: Writing Seminar, Culture and Difference, Epistemology and
Cognition, Ethical Thought and Moral Values, Historical
Analysis, and Quantitative and Computational Reasoning. For the requirement in Language, the number of
required courses depends on proficiency. Three areas require two courses: Literature and the Arts, Science and
Engineering, and Social Analysis.

Princeton argues that the university's general education distribution requirements "represent different ways
of knowing, all of which . . . are essential for educated citizenship." Like other universities that have chosen distribution requirements, Princeton states that "exposure
to a variety of academic disciplines not only helps [stu-
dents] identify the right intellectual tools for the task at

hand but also deepens [their] respect for the variety of ways human beings seek to understand our world." The general education requirements also "offer students the chance to develop both intellectual rigor and humility by considering the possibilities and limitations of all forms of academic inquiry."

As in most of the Ivy League, Princeton's broad distribution requirements risk leaving students with a fragmented and incomplete education. Students will need to choose their courses wisely to get a strong education, while those who want to slide through Princeton without friction can easily escape rigorous courses.

WRITING SEMINAR

Each writing seminar has a common goal for students: "through practice and guidance, to master essential strategies and techniques of college-level inquiry and argument." The options usually differ by semester, with only some courses reappearing after previous semesters. This churn is good news for serious students since no course examined for this book is suitable for them.

This academic year, Princeton offers thirty-seven seminars for the fall semester and repeats them in the spring. The worst among them are:

- Assigned at Birth: "How gender is taught, embodied, resisted, redefined, and policed."
- Body Matters: "How we observe, treat, and manipulate the human form." Students must "choose a phenomenon or controversy involving the body's physical form and craft an original argument placing it in a cultural, political, or scientific context. Examples may include TSA body scanners, bans on gender-affirming healthcare, vaccine debates, eighteenth-century grave-robbing, body artists like ORLAN, and *Frankenstein*."

- Disability Justice: Students explore "the contentious scholarly debate about medical and social models of disability in light of the historic Disability Rights Movement" and the "often elusive concept of disability justice in the context of scholarship on racism, neoliberalism, universal design, and assistive technology."
- Educational Equities: Students "develop an original argument about equity in education." Some possible topics are "grading systems, student loans, and digital learning platforms."
- Modern Love: This course begins with "Weike Wang's short story about a woman whose boyfriend complains that she is constantly overthinking everything, examining it through the lens of Kate Manne's philosophy of gaslighting."
- Real Fakes: Students "explore people and artifacts that blur the line between reality and falsity." Potential research topics include "advancements in plastic surgery, the economics of counterfeit and dupe products, frauds like Anna Delvey and Elizabeth Holmes, the staying power of conspiracy theories, no-makeup makeup and the clean girl aesthetic, reality television, Münchausen syndrome, and catfishing."
- Sexual Revolutions: Students "investigate the perpetual tension between cultural evolution and institutional stasis, and we do so by exploring some of the most cherished parts of our personal lives: gendered identities and sexual intimacies."
- Bad Botany: Students "research a plant of their choosing in the context of a specific social or climate justice movement, economic project, or colonial encounter."

Those were among the options listed in mid-2024. The authors hope better options became available for students in Spring 2025.

LANGUAGE

Students must complete one to four courses "depending on the language students study and the level at which they start," and students are expected to develop proficiency in a language by the end of their junior year.

Princeton students can choose from a wide variety of language courses, including German, French, Ancient Greek, Arabic, Hebrew, Italian, Japanese, Korean, Portuguese, Russian, Swahili, Turkish, Ukrainian, Urdu, and more.

CULTURE AND DIFFERENCE

Culture and Difference courses "use cultural analysis to trace [how] human beings construct meaning both within and across groups." In addition, the courses should offer students a "lens through which other forms of disciplinary inquiry are enhanced, critiqued, and clarified, often paying close attention to the experiences and perspectives of groups who have historically been excluded from dominant cultural narratives or structures of social power." Almost one hundred courses are available.

This distribution requirement is unique in that it may be "satisfied independently or concurrently with another distribution area." In short, students can essentially avoid this distribution area by taking an additional course that meets a different distribution requirement. That strategy may be worthwhile for a serious Princeton student, considering these many underwhelming options:

- Topics in African American Culture and Life: Black Disability Studies, Black Disability Histories: This course "challenges the racial parameters of disability studies and disability history by asking how persistent conditions of antiblack violence, including mass incarceration, state divestment, medical neglect, and environmental racism, destabilize assumptions about what constitutes an 'able body.'" Students also "recover disability theories that are already intrinsic to the Black radical tradition, postcolonial studies, and Black feminisms."

- Regarding the Pain of Others: "Drawing from critical race theories, queer and psychoanalytic theories, and transnational feminist work, this course analyzes pain/violence narratives from a wide range of genres—film, essay, memoir, and policy—to explore how pain and violence [are] narrated and depicted and how such narrations become part of a collective consciousness that keeps systematic forms of oppression intact."

- Critical Native American and Indigenous Studies [NAIS]: Students hear that "Princeton University is on the unceded ancestral lands of the Lenape people, who endure to this day." The course discusses "settler colonialism, Indigenous knowledge, resistance, education, research, stereotypes and cultural appropriation, identity, nation (re)building, and critiques of NAIS."

- Justice: This class will explore "how justice is defined and sought by looking at criminality, fights for Indigenous and women's rights, post-conflict transitions, environmental catastrophe, debates about reparations, and intimate forms of repair." The reading list includes *The Case for Reparations* (Ta-Nahesi Coates), *Reproductive Injustice* (Dána-Ain Davis), and "Decolonization is not a Metaphor" (Eve Tuck and K. Wayne Yang).

- Queer Becomings: "What is the relationship between queerness and larger forces such as culture, coloniality, global capitalism, religion, and the state?"

- Gender and the Household: Students will "ground their work in historical and ethnographic research on the connections between colonialism, chattel slavery, capitalism, and gender, sexual relations, and the family."

- The Poetics and Politics of Pronouns: The course

"investigates the history of theoretical reflection on and
literary experimentation with pronouns." Students also
consider, "How do pronouns regulate our relation to the
world, to one another, and to gender?"

- Thinking with Bad Bunny: [T]he Cultural Politics of
Race, Language, and Empire: In this course, with an
"interdisciplinary lens," students "engage in a critical
analysis of [rapper Bad Bunny's] music, lyrics, aesthetics, activism, gender non-conforming performances,
and savvy business strategies." Take heart, friends of
Princeton—things could be worse—Cornell's curriculum includes Cardi B.

A serious student does, however, have some good options:

- What is a Classic? The course examines "four monumental poems from the ancient Mediterranean and Near East:
Homer's *Iliad* and *Odyssey*, Virgil's *Aeneid*, and *Gilgamesh*,
which are discussed through comparison across traditions, ranging as far as Chinese poetry."
- History of the American West, 1500–1999: This course
treats "the US West's place, process, idea, cultural memory, conquest, and legacies throughout American history."
- Hellenism: The First 3,000 Years: Students "trace the
history of these two phenomena: the political life and
fortunes of Greek speakers and the cultural life of texts
written in Greek, seeking to understand the relationship
between the two."
- Introduction to African Literature and Film: Students
study "the richness and diversity of foundational African
texts (some in translation) while foregrounding questions of aesthetics, style, humor, [and] epistemology."

EPISTEMOLOGY AND COGNITION

Epistemology and Cognition courses "address the nature
and limits of human knowledge" and have the goal of

"encouraging students to reflect on the linguistic, psychological, and cultural structures that make knowledge possible." Forty courses meet this requirement, and many of them overlap with courses listed in other distribution areas. The two to avoid are:

- Empire of the Ark: Animals and Environments in Film, Photography, and Popular Culture: This course "explores the fascination with animals in film, photography and popular culture, engaging critical issues in animal and environmental studies."
- Topics in Critical Theory: Philosophy and the Irrational: This course attempts to "scrutinize the jargons of authenticity and interiority in a range of current cultural discourses while adding new perspectives from feminist theory, new materialism, and aesthetics."

In contrast, wise students should choose one of these:

- Philosophy and the Modern Mind: This course is a "historical introduction to philosophy since 1600, emphasizing close reading of classic texts, but including some attention to the scientific, religious, political, literary, and other contexts."
- Introduction to Language and Linguistics: This course is an "introduction to the scientific analysis of the structure and uses of language."

ETHICAL THOUGHT AND MORAL VALUES

Courses in Ethical Thought and Moral Values equip students to "understand the basis of their own moral reasoning and ethical issues as they arise in social life while cultivating the possibility of a common ethical language among people whose traditions and values differ." More than forty courses meet the requirement this term.

Among the worse options are:

- The Anthropology of Law: "How can the anthropology of law help us to better understand past and present ideas of justice and be a mobilizing force in the quest for social and environmental justice?"
- Introduction to Feminist Political Philosophy: The course opens with a declaration: "Sexism, misogyny, and gender injustice are grave moral and political wrongs." Students consider, "What is oppression? What is sexism? What is gender? How does intersectionality complicate our understanding of these questions?"
- Just Transitions and Climate Futures: This course "traces the historical origins and contested uses of just transition frameworks, exploring debates and common ground among labor, policy, environmental justice, ecosocialist, and decolonial perspectives."
- Anthropology and Environment: This course "explores anthropology's engagement with environmental questions, beyond binaries of 'nature' and 'culture.'" Topics include "climate, materiality, cosmologies, more-than-human ethnography, and environmental justice."
- Types of Ideology and Literary Form: Ethics, the Novel, and Pornography: This seminar course "considers how the Enlightenment idea of 'moral character,' as something understood and engendered through reading, connects the emergence of both pornography and the novel as distinct categories of representation in Europe." *Fifty Shades of Gray* is on the reading list.
- Coming to Our Senses: Climate Justice—Climate Change in Film, Photography, and Popular Culture: "The vital ways environmental issues intersect with gender, race, and sexualities."
- The Just Society: An "introduction to theories of social justice and examination of their implications in areas of contemporary social and political controversy."

The better options are these:

- Political Theory: Students review the writings of "ancient
  and modern theorists, including Aristotle, Machiavelli,
  Montesquieu, and the American Founders." Students also
  "seek to understand important concepts such as virtue,
  moderation, justice, and order."
- East Asian Humanities I: The Classical Foundations: An
  "introduction to the literature, art, religion, and philosophy of China, Japan, and Korea from antiquity to
  c. 1600."

HISTORICAL ANALYSIS

Historical Analysis courses invite students to "enter imag-
inatively into languages, institutions, and worldviews of
the past." They also ask students to make "critical judgments about the conclusions we can draw from the traces
of the past to which we have access."

Nearly one hundred courses are available to meet this
requirement. Many of them overlap with courses listed
in other distribution areas.

Among the worst options:

- Topics in African American Culture and Life: Black
  Disability Studies, Black Disability Histories (described
  above).
- Critical Native American and Indigenous Studies (described above).
- Histories of Anthropological Theory: This course "begins
  with a discussion of the current state of affairs in anthropological theory . . . and includes situating anthropological theory within the context of social and political
  theory and seeing how post-structuralism, post-colonial
  theory, black studies, and feminism reshaped the discipline in a variety of ways."
- Magic and Witchcraft in the Ancient World: Students

"investigate ancient ideas about magic, alternative divine powers, and the relationship between practitioners and clients in this system."

- Why Weimar Now? Material Culture and Historical Analogy: This course explores "the negative political analogy between pre-fascist Weimar and our time: the US as a 'new Weimar,' 'the crisis of parliamentary democracy,' the rise of White Supremacy, the 'agitator,' and the danger of pluralization."

- Understanding the Recent Queer Past: "An intensive introduction to working with cultural documents emerging within and from LGBTQ+ communities in the United States during the late twentieth and early twenty-first centuries."

- 'Cult' Controversies in America: Students "pay particular attention to government and media constructions of the religious mainstream and margin, to the politics of labels such as 'cult' and 'sect,' to race, gender, and sexuality within new religions, and to the role of American law in constructing categories and shaping religious expressions."

Fortunately, Princeton students also have several better choices:

- World Art History: The "art of different cultures and continents throughout the world from the first civilizations to the present."

- The Roman Republic: "The development of Roman society, the rise and fall of republican government, and the Republic's many afterlives."

- Introduction to Classics: In this seminar course, "students will become acquainted with different fields of study within the [Classics] Department, including literature, ancient history, linguistics, and the long reception of antiquity in the Middle Ages and modernity."

- The Byzantine Empire: This course "explores one of the greatest civilizations the world has known, tracing the experiences of its majority and minority groups through the dramatic centuries of the Islamic conquests, Iconoclasm, and the Crusades, until its final fall to the Ottoman Turks."
- British Empire in World History, 1600–2000: This course "focuses on England, Wales, Scotland, and Ireland, and the Empire these peoples generated after c. 1600, and uses this as a lens through which to examine the phenomenon of empire more broadly."

LITERATURE AND THE ARTS

Unlike other distribution requirements, two courses are required to satisfy the Literature and the Arts requirement. Here, students may "produce creative, imaginative works or practice interpreting them." Students may also "choreograph dances or read Shakespeare's plays or create performance pieces that use imaginative and interpretive skills critically and physically."

More than 250 courses can satisfy this requirement, and many of them overlap with courses listed in other distribution areas.

Princeton slackers have many options to avoid rigorous academic work:

- The Political Lives of Angela Davis: This pro-Marxist hagiography is "organized around readings of Davis's robust body of her life's work, including essays written while she was imprisoned and books that have become foundational in feminist scholarship."
- Climate Storytelling for Climate Action: This course "explores climate stories to ask how they can lead to meaningful action."
- Queer Visions: Transcending Borders through Film and Visual Culture: This course will "center a transnational,

intersectional, and comparative perspective that will allow us to think about multiple social movements, styles, and aesthetics while centering the lives of people who have experienced the cost of homophobia, transphobia, and misogyny often while fighting against other forms of colonized oppression such as racism and poverty."

- Topics in Critical Theory: Frantz Fanon: "Decolonization, infrastructural critique, systemic racism, existentialist phenomenology, *négritude*, violence, dialectics, psychiatry (vs. psychoanalysis), national consciousness, revolution, poesis, praxis."

- Environmental Film Studies: Research Film Studio: Students "experiment with a possible compromise between the civilizational paradigms of settler colonialism vs. nomadic homelessness."

- Decadence: Empire, Sexuality, Aesthetics: Students explore "[t]he foreigner, the pervert, the outcast . . . figures at the margins of the social order, who are valorized and exalted."

- *Manga*: Visual Culture in Modern Japan: "This course examines the comic book [*Manga*] as an expressive medium in Japan."

- Introduction to Ballet: Students "learn the fundamentals of ballet, understanding its physicality, artistry, and principles of alignment." Like some other courses listed here, this one is valuable in itself, but not in lieu of an academically rigorous core course.

- Princeton Dance Festival: Choreography and Performance: Students "learn and perform dances through collaboration with faculty or by learning significant dances from contemporary choreographers."

- Princeton Atelier: Baby Wants Candy: Creating Comedy for Television: This course "will explore the creation of a television comedy led by Al Samuels (*Sports Action Team*) and Allison Silverman (*The Daily Show, Unbreakable Kimmy Schmidt, Late Night*)."

Three classes, in contrast, stand out for serious students:

- What is a Classic? (This course is described above.)
- Shakespeare: Toward *Hamlet*: Students study "the first half of Shakespeare's career, with a focus on the great comedies and histories of the 1590s, culminating in a study of *Hamlet*."
- Topics in Medieval Italian Literature and Culture: Writing Latin in Late Medieval Italy: This course "focuses on the close reading in the original Latin of a wide selection of thirteenth- and fourteenth-century Italian writers of hagiographic texts, Church documents, scientific inquiries, epic poetry, as well as of treatises about linguistics, poetics, ethics, and historiography." *Mirabile dictu*, that's a serious academic agenda indeed.

QUANTITATIVE AND COMPUTATIONAL REASONING

Quantitative and Computational Reasoning courses "engage students in the logic of mathematics and the manipulation of numerical and categorical information." About ninety courses meet the requirement.

As at several institutions, one of the easiest ways to fulfill the requirement is to learn a bit more about our solar system. Planets in the Universe does the trick. It's an "introductory course in astronomy focusing on planets in our Solar System and around other stars (exoplanets)." This course has no prerequisites past high-school algebra and geometry.

The rest of the options serve Princeton well. Indeed, almost all courses listed under the Quantitative and Computational Reasoning distribution requirement are worthwhile and academically challenging. Consider these:

- Introduction to Environmental Engineering: This course "introduces the basic chemical and physical processes relevant to environmental engineering."

- Computer Science: An Interdisciplinary Approach: The course "uses Java programming to introduce fundamental programming concepts, including conditionals, loops, arrays, functions, and object-oriented programming."
- Algorithms and Data Structures: This course "surveys the most important algorithms and data structures in use on computers today."
- Statistics and Data Analysis for Economics: "An introduction to probability and statistical methods for empirical work in economics."
- An Integrated, Quantitative Introduction to Life Sciences: A sequence of four courses that "integrates introductory topics in calculus-based physics, chemistry, molecular biology, and scientific computing with Python, with an emphasis on laboratory experimentation, quantitative reasoning, and data-oriented thinking."
- History of Mathematics: Students study "some of the most beautiful and timeless mathematical problems and solutions (theorems and proofs) and their discoverers, as well as the historical developments that led to each breakthrough."
- Probability Theory: This course introduces probability theory "and begins with the measure-theoretic foundations of probability theory, expectation, distributions, and limit theorems."
- Fundamentals of Statistics: A "first introduction to probability and statistics." The course "will provide background to understand and produce rigorous statistical analysis including estimation, confidence intervals, hypothesis testing, and regression and classification."

Additionally, Calculus I, Calculus II, and Multivariable Calculus are offered in multiple sections.

SCIENCE AND ENGINEERING

Students must complete two courses to satisfy the Science and Engineering distribution requirement. At least one course "must be a science and engineering course with laboratory (SEL)." Students may also "elect a second laboratory science course, or a non-laboratory science course (SEN)." There were forty-one SEL courses and forty-three SEN courses in the Fall 2024 semester.

It's easy to avoid serious academic development in science and engineering or to indulge one's predilection for climate change negativity. Slackers should consider these courses:

- (SEN) Physics for Future Leaders: This course "is designed for non-scientists who will someday become our informed citizens and decision-makers."
- (SEL) The Kitchen Lab: Food and Health: Students learn how to "prepare foods like hummus, falafel, *manakish za'atar* and [how] to make cheese, yogurt, pickles, kombucha, and much more!"
- (SEL) A Perfect Cup of Coffee: Students "work in groups to brew the best tasting cup of coffee with the minimum amount of energy."
- (SEL) Musical Instruments, Sound, Perception, and Creativity: Students learn how "musical instruments reside at the intersection of varied topics: sound, perception, embodiment, music theory, social values, and more."
- (SEN) Ecosystems, Climate Change, and Global Food: Students "examine fundamental methods of analyzing ecosystems and apply these methods to questions about climate change and the global food system."
- (SEN) Scientific Foundations of the Environmental Nexus: "The scientific and technological dimensions of the nexus of global environmental problems: climate change, the carbon cycle, biodiversity loss, and the provision of food and water."

- (SEL) Climate: Past, Present, and Future: "Which human activities are changing our climate, and does climate change constitute a major problem?"

It's also easy to find academic rigor:

- (SEN) Introduction to Chemical and Biochemical Engineering Principles: An introduction to "the principles underlying chemical and biochemical engineering."
- (SEN) The Quantum World: An introduction to quantum mechanics "for students interested in its relevance to chemistry, emphasizing fundamental and conceptual understanding."
- (SEN) Biochemistry: The "fundamental concepts of biomolecular structure and function will be discussed, emphasizing principles of thermodynamics, binding, and catalysis."
- (SEN) Fundamentals of Neuroscience: This course is an "intensive introduction to fundamental topics in neuroscience, including neuronal excitability, synaptic physiology, neural networks, and circuits that mediate perception, action, emotion, and memory."
- (SEN) Thermal Physics: An introduction to "thermodynamics and statistical mechanics, both classical and quantum."

Additional strong options are in general chemistry, organic chemistry, contemporary logic design (regarding computation and communication circuits), foundations of engineering, thermodynamics, and other truly challenging areas.

SOCIAL ANALYSIS

Students must complete two courses to satisfy the Social Analysis distribution requirement. The 135 available Social Analysis courses "involve the study of the structures, processes, and meanings human beings create through our interactions with one another, and the networks and institutions through which human behavior develops and evolves."

Slackers should take any two of these (a few options described above are omitted here):

- Shoes: This narrow course teaches how "shoes have refocused our attention on issues of ethics and morality. Shoes are a window into our personal and collective history and future."
- Justice: "How justice is defined and sought by looking at criminality, fights for indigenous and women's rights, post-conflict transitions, environmental catastrophe, debates about reparations, and intimate forms of repair."
- Violence: "Conquest and colonialism, genocidal violence, state violence and political resistance, everyday violence, gendered violence, racialization, torture, as well as witnessing and repair."
- Ethnography, Evidence, and Experience: Students "acquire the tools to theorize social experience, develop new approaches to power, memory, and history, and probe the potentials for decolonial and anticolonial scholarship."
- Anthropologies of Climate and Change: Students "explore climate as a keyword to consider nihilism, hope, new and old fantasies of engineering, and unexpected imaginaries of planetary resilience or collapse."
- GLAMbasted: Cultural Heritage Institutions Under Fire: Students explore how "the GLAM sector (galleries, libraries, archives, and museums) is in defense mode today, facing book bans, protests, and critique from all sides."
- The Coming of Driverless Cars: This course "helps students see the changing globalized world through the lens of driverless cars."

- What's Your Sign? This course "explores the cultural history of popular tools that we use to define the self, from horoscopes to Myers-Briggs questionnaires and Buzzfeed personality tests."
- Body Politics: Pro Wrestling in Social, Cultural, and Political Perspective: This course safely, from a distance, helps students "study the practice of pro wrestling from different theoretical perspectives, including the cultural-comparative, phenomenological, social constructionist, artistic, labor-economic, and political."
- Introduction to Gender and Sexuality Studies: "How do gender and sexuality emerge from networks of power and social relations?"

The Department of Economics, with a boost from political science, rescues students looking for a serious way to take two worthwhile courses, particularly these:

- Introduction to Microeconomics: Exactly as advertised.
- Introduction to Macroeconomics: This course is also precisely what it says it is.
- Microeconomic Theory: This course builds on the knowledge of microeconomics from the Introduction to Microeconomics course.
- Law and Economics: An "introduction to the economics of law."
- Financial Investments: This course "provides an overview of financial markets and instruments, including stocks, bonds, futures, options, and other derivatives."

There's also Constitutional Interpretation: A "study of the structure of the American constitutional system and the meaning of key constitutional provisions." Note well that Professor Robert P. George, the Director of the James Madison Program in American Ideals and Institutions, teaches this class. Princeton Tigers, don't miss it.

Conclusion

Princeton's general education requirements, encompassing eight distribution areas alongside writing and language components, are similar to those of most other Ivy League universities. Students at Princeton have considerable flexibility in selecting courses to fulfill these requirements. This means that a student's educational experience can vary significantly, not merely on the basis of individual interests, but also on the basis of the seriousness and rigor of the courses chosen.

Indeed, the absence of a core curriculum—what's here offers little vision of the educated Princeton Man or Princeton Woman—makes it easy for an undergraduate to leave the university without a well-rounded or academically rigorous education. Even so, a well-advised student can pursue an excellent education worthy of Princeton's name.

It should be evident to the reader which of these two paths at Princeton is the worthier.

Option #1

SOCIAL ANALYSIS

- Shoes
- What's Your Sign?

CULTURE AND DIFFERENCE

- The Poetics and Politics of Pronouns

EPISTEMOLOGY AND COGNITION

- Empire of the Ark

ETHICAL THOUGHT AND MORAL VALUES

- Introduction to Feminist Political Philosophy

HISTORICAL ANALYSIS

- Topics in African American Culture and Life: Black Disability Studies, Black Disability Histories

LITERATURE AND THE ARTS

- Topics in Critical Theory: Frantz Fanon
- The Political Lives of Angela Davis

QUANTITATIVE AND COMPUTATIONAL REASONING

- Planets in the Universe

SCIENCE AND ENGINEERING

- A Perfect Cup of Coffee
- Ecosystems, Climate Change, and Global Food

WRITING SEMINAR AND FOREIGN LANGUAGE

- Modern Love
- French

Option #2

SOCIAL ANALYSIS

- Introduction to Microeconomics
- Constitutional Interpretation

CULTURE AND DIFFERENCE

- What is a Classic?

EPISTEMOLOGY AND COGNITION

- Introduction to Language and Linguistics

ETHICAL THOUGHT AND MORAL VALUES

- Political Theory

HISTORICAL ANALYSIS

- The Roman Republic

LITERATURE AND THE ARTS

- Shakespeare: Toward *Hamlet*
- Topics in Medieval Italian Literature and Culture

QUANTITATIVE AND COMPUTATIONAL REASONING

- Statistics and Data Analysis for Economics

SCIENCE AND ENGINEERING

- General Chemistry I
- Thermal Physics

WRITING SEMINAR

- [Hope for a good course to become available.]

LANGUAGE

- Introduction to Ancient Greek

DARTMOUTH COLLEGE

U ndergraduates of Dartmouth College must fulfill general academic requirements in order to
graduate, in addition to the credits required to
complete a major. The requirements include some particular to first-year students, as well as broad area requirements that can be fulfilled throughout a student's college
career. Dartmouth also requires the completion of three
terms of physical or wellness education (or one, for college athletes) and a fifty-yard swim test.

FIRST-YEAR WRITING REQUIREMENTS

Dartmouth requires all students to take two or three
writing-focused courses in their first year, depending on a
faculty recommendation and self-placement. In the fall or
winter term, students must take a general writing course
(or two-term sequence) introducing them to "critical writing," which Dartmouth defines as the "practice of thinking by means of which ideas are discovered, examined,
compared, evaluated, refined, and promoted." Course
descriptions promise intensive writing assignments, including peer reviews and draft revisions. In the following
term, students proceed with a required first-year seminar
"designed both to further the student's proficiency in
writing and to provide an opportunity for participation

in small group study and discussions with an instructor on a subject of mutual interest." Both the introductory writing courses and the first-year seminars limit enrollment to sixteen students per class, guaranteeing students at least two small classes in their first year at Dartmouth.

The readings for most of the introductory writing courses (Writing 5 and Writing 2-3) change with the instructor. As an alternative to Writing 5 or Writing 2-3, students may take Global Humanities 1, part of the Humanities Sequence, a "selective, interdisciplinary, two-term sequence for up to one hundred first-year students." Readings for Global Humanities 1 also vary from year to year, and this year's strong iteration features texts by Sophocles, Tolstoy, Nietzsche, Marx, and Rawls.

The Fall 2024 course descriptions were not on Dartmouth's website as we prepared this chapter, but the Winter 2024 Writing 5 section descriptions were available. These are much weaker than the Global Humanities 1 options, and they range from lackluster and generic to identity-focused. Among the least impressive academically were:

- Representing Autism and Neurodiversity, in which central course questions include, "How have race, gender, and sexuality been included (or excluded) from our understanding of neurodivergent identity?" and "What is the neurodiversity movement and how has it shifted the conversation?"
- Image and Text, in which readings include "ekphrastic poetry, graphic novels, advertisements, [and] political cartoons."
- The Relationships Between Language, Culture, and Thought, with course "texts" consisting of academic articles, TED talks, podcasts, and academic conference presentations.
- Future Fantasies: Imagining the Posthuman, which

considers the relationship between fictionalized representations of the future and "our real processes of 'othering' across cultures, ethnicities, and genders.'"

- Performing Gender, which takes as its starting point the asserted truth that gender "is an embodied social category that governs the ways we become legible in society from birth, yet is also a powerful site of liberation, self-determination, and experimentation."

Writing 5 topics with greater academic heft were wanting but included "Einstein's Universe," which considered the concept of time in modern physics.

The readings and topics for first-year seminars also vary with the instructor, and Global Humanities 2, the second part of the Humanities Sequence, may also satisfy the requirement. The preliminary reading list for this year's iteration includes classic works ranging from Shakespeare's *Romeo and Juliet* and Nathaniel Hawthorne's *The Scarlet Letter* to Miguel de Cervantes's *The Stage of Wonders* and Anton Chekhov's *Uncle Vanya*.

Unfortunately, descriptions of the other first-year seminars are not nearly as impressive. Though hot topics concerning race, gender, and climate change dominate the Spring 2024 section descriptions, a couple of seminars at least have the virtue of framing the course as a "debate." Consider the following:

- He, She, or It: Reconstructing Gender in Science Fiction takes as its starting point the truth that "one cannot fully appreciate the significance of feminism and its influences on social change without considering other closely related issues of race and ethnicity, social class, and sexual orientation through an 'intersectional' lens."
- More-Than-Human Narratives: Posthumanism, Ecocriticism, Animal Studies: Topics include "anthropocentric normativity," "human ontological privilege," "unified

natureculture [sic]," "material ecocriticism," and, of course, "animal studies."

- Cultures of Self-Loathing: The course to take to investigate how self-loathing plays "a hidden role in politics that includes racism, sexism, body shaming, and so on."
- War and Colonialism in Asian American Literature: Topics include "settler colonialism, militarism, Orientalism, transnational and transracial adoption, transnational decolonial feminism, queer of color critique, critical race and ethnic studies, and Indigenous studies."
- Fact or Fiction? Politicized Topics in Biology: "The majority of the course will be focused on written and oral debates on topics including: climate change, genetic engineering, vaccine safety, and antibiotic resistance."
- Debates in Ecosocialism: "[T]he course will delve into debates regarding why ecosocialism is necessary, how political movements can pursue radical change, how and why social difference matters, and how an ecosocialist economy should conceptualize its relationship to growth and technology."
- Climate Change: A course on "the nature and cause of climate change, potential impacts on us, and the implications for our nation's energy issues."
- The Female Detective asks what happens "when the historically male sleuth is replaced by a female detective?" Readings include selections from "the sub-genre of queer/lesbian detection."
- Picturing African American: Students explore the "ethics of historical illustration" and "learn to think analytically about the racial implications of the visual histories they encounter."
- Coloring Brazil: Representations and Self-Representations of Afro-Brazilian Descendants: The course asks, "How [do] social activism and the black movement in Brazil intertwine with artistic practices and

fictional representations?" and, inevitably, "How race intersects with other axes of oppression such as gender and class."

- Theater for Social Change: think *activism*, but make it artsy.
- Managing Emotions: "Drawing on insights from sociology to psychotherapy, this is an interdisciplinary course on managing one's emotions."
- Reimagining the Myth: Paris in Literature and Film: "What roles do gender, culture, immigration, and economic status play in incubating these identities in this particular, almost mythically idealized place?"
- Animal Musics: "This first-year seminar takes selected topics in animal 'musics' and humanity's interest in them for the purpose of learning how professional non-fiction authors, journalists, and academic humanities scholars engage US audiences in new ideas and new research about music through their writing."

More serious options include:

- Paris in the Nineteenth Century: A robust art history seminar examining the modernization of Paris and its impact on modern art—Realism, Impressionism, and Post-Impressionism—as well as on photography, sculpture, architecture, and film.
- The Art of Human Dialogue: Is dialogue unique to humans? In the age of AI chatbots, this course examines ancient and modern dialogues to better understand how AI-generated dialogue "compares to its human counterpart, and what about that most excites and concerns us."
- Athens to the Americas: "We will explore the life and legacy of the ancient plays about Medea in the plays and films of Latin America."
- Early American Feminism: "This seminar will examine the early history of feminism in the United States,

investigating the foundational ideas that animated it, the striking context in which it emerged, and the complicated legacy it has entailed."

- Toni Morrison: An "in-depth study of Toni Morrison's major fictional works."

LANGUAGE REQUIREMENT

All undergraduates must complete the language requirement by taking any language taught at Dartmouth up through the 03 level and, beginning with the class of 2026, Dartmouth no longer permits undergraduates to "test out" of the requirement. Instead, students who demonstrate some level of competency through a local placement test may either continue the language of competency at a more advanced level or start a new language. Dartmouth offers courses in thirteen languages, ranging from Arabic to Ukrainian.

General Education Requirements

Dartmouth organizes its general education requirements into two groups—Distributive Requirements and World Culture Requirements—though all of the college's requirements follow the "distributional" approach of permitting students to choose from hundreds of course options to fulfill each requirement. Most subject and proficiency areas require one course, with the exceptions of Social Analysis and Natural and Physical Science, which each require two. Since some courses count towards both a World Culture requirement and a Distributive requirement, a student can satisfy the thirteen requirements below with just ten courses.

DISTRIBUTIVE REQUIREMENTS

- Art courses aim to foster creativity, artistic skills, and the "interpretive powers that will allow [students] to be informed participants in the world of the arts and contemporary media."
- Literature can include English courses as well as literature courses taught in other languages, with the goal of developing "knowledge and appreciation of literary texts," as well as "literary criticism."
- Systems and Traditions of Thought, Meaning, and Value includes courses in government and sociology as well as philosophy and religion to examine "such topics as the meaning of human existence and the nature of truth, knowledge, or morality."
- International or Comparative Study considers "interrelationships among societies, cultures, or nations and/or the methods or approaches employed in comparative studies," with topics heavy on colonialism, imperialism, and identity.
- Social Analysis courses mostly stem from the social sciences, with ample opportunities for the study of intersectionality.
- Quantitative and Deductive Science is the math requirement.
- Natural and Physical Science ensures that all Dartmouth graduates understand "the basic principles and terminology of science," and "the ways in which scientists obtain, validate, judge, test, and then re-judge information."
- Technology or Applied Science courses "must include the methodology and theory of applied science" to "enable students to understand the process by which the discoveries of basic science have been translated into products, facilities, services, devices, and technical information."

WORLD CULTURE REQUIREMENTS

- Western Cultures, which includes the "cultures of the classical Judeo-Christian and Greco-Roman Mediterranean, and of Europe and its settlements."
- Non-Western Cultures, "including those with a history of colonialism."
- Culture and Identity is less focused on culture than it is on identities, including those "defined by race, gender, sexuality, class, religion, and ethnicity."

Here are some standout courses in each area, courses either to take or to avoid. Course offerings vary from term to term and year to year, and the examples below draw from the Fall 2024 offerings.

ART (ART)

More than one hundred courses offered this fall fulfill the Art requirement, with more than half of them focused on instruction in the practice of an artistic discipline for its own sake, whether in music, theatre, or a visual art. Unfortunately, plenty of options remain for those hoping to put art in the service of activism:

- Music and Social Justice: "This course asks what we can do for music and what music can do for the world."
- Food and Art: Global History: Topics include "plastics and lunchboxes," the "pop art of food," "activist food art," and more.
- Queer Cinema: "What constitutes queer aesthetics and politics today?"
- Ecology and Art in Oceania: "In the context of these histories of environmental destruction, the course will embrace and explore Indigenous artistic activism."
- Art and Activism: "This course will look at various international and domestic artists to examine how

contemporary visual art can be a form of social activism."
- Many Faces of Brazilian Cinema: Topics include "The Other's gaze in Brazil," "reassessment of African and indigenous roots," and "representations of race and gender."

For students hoping to deepen their appreciation of art outside of the studio and without a heavy dose of politics, options include:

- Art in Ancient Greece: from sculpture to architecture.
- Sacred Architecture of Asia: Case studies include "Buddhist monasteries, Hindu temples, Mosques, Daoist and Confucian temples, [and] Shinto shrines."
- Art and Aesthetics: a philosophy course on the meaning of art and beauty.

LITERATURE (LIT)

More than fifty courses offered this fall fulfill the Literature requirement, and they include an impressive array of reading lists spanning a range of Western and Eastern classical literature. Though a handful of course topics manage to snag the "LIT" designation without actually focusing on literature, and a few infuse "oppression" studies, most appear rigorous. See the lowlights and highlights below.

Lowlights:

- Environmental Crises and Human Rights: Literature takes a back seat in this course to the "violence" of flooding, drought, and wildfires "playing out in locations already plagued with inequalities and human rights violations."
- Read the World: "Do you know how to read? Faces. Words. Pictures. Bodies. Games. Books. People." Literature again takes a back seat as readings draw from "various media: text, movies, video games, *anime*, and digital arts."

- Ghosts, Monsters, Psychos: "The techniques filmmakers in Japan, Europe, and the Americas have used to create an aesthetics of horror."
- Contemporary Native American Poetry: "The indigenous poetic voice occupies a unique position in contemporary American poetry, but also in the discourse of settler colonialism."
- Black German Writers: This course, taught in German, "map[s] Black German literature, from poems and rap songs to short stories and novels, between the 1980s to the present."

Highlights:

- *The Tale of Genji*: A course on a classic work of Japanese literature, possibly the world's first novel.
- Souls Sold to the Devil: Cheeky title aside, the subject matter is serious, concentrating on the famous story of Faust as told in Marlowe's *The Tragical History of the Life and Death of Doctor Faustus*, Goethe's *Faust*, and Mann's *Doctor Faustus*.
- James Joyce's *Ulysses*: True to its title, this course is a close reading of James Joyce's novel, happily focusing more on literature than literary critics—"for the most part our primary text will be Joyce's own words— wherever they lead us."
- Dostoevsky: Problem of Evil probes "the tragedy of human existence" as well as the "terrifying isolation of a human being separated from God" in *Notes from Underground*, *Crime and Punishment*, *The Idiot*, *Demons*, and, of course, *The Brothers Karamazov*.
- Helen in Greek Literature: Learn about "one of the most elusive and enchanting figures of Greek antiquity" in works by Homer, Sappho, Herodotus, Euripides, and Plutarch.

SYSTEMS AND TRADITIONS OF THOUGHT,
MEANING, AND VALUE

Roughly forty courses offered this fall fulfill the Systems
and Traditions of Thought, Meaning, and Value requirement. While not all course options "provide students
with systematic, critical understanding of philosophical
issues or systems of religious belief or practice," some appear poised to do so well. The weakest options include:

- Jews and Race: With such a rich Jewish tradition of
  thought, meaning, and value, it's a shame this course opts
  to focus on "the question of race." Topics include "the complex alliance of Jews and Blacks from slavery to BLM," "the
  role of race in the Israeli/Palestinian conflict," and "the rise
  of Islamophobia," as well as whether Jews are "white."
- Video Games and the Meaning of Life "explores the modern human condition through the stories, designs, and
  soundscapes of digital games."
- Philosophy and Gender: "Is knowledge gendered? Is
  value gendered? What is a (gendered) self?"

Stronger options, however, include:

- Confrontations with Death: This French course examines "the relationship of death to the history of French
  culture and the philosophical traditions it embodies,"
  including texts from Montaigne, Pascal, Sartre, Derrida,
  and more.
- Political Ideas: This political theory survey course covers
  political philosophers ranging from Plato and Augustine
  to Rousseau and Nietzsche.
- Religion of Israel: Hebrew Bible: Course readings include
  Genesis, Exodus, Joshua, Samuel, the Psalms, Job, and the
  prophets.
- Reproductive Ethics: This course tackles controversial
  questions head-on, but appears poised to approach them

in the spirit of genuine inquiry, asking questions including, "What may we do in the interest of creating human life?" and "What do we owe human life, once it has begun to develop?"

- Beauty: A philosophical inquiry into beauty, drawing from thinkers such as Aristotle, Plotinus, Shaftesbury, and Schiller.

INTERNATIONAL OR COMPARATIVE STUDY

Ideally, comparative studies should raise questions about first principles: Given the existence of different regimes and ways of life, which are best? Do some differences matter more than others, and if so, why? Instead of raising these questions, however, many of the ninety course options presume answers from the outset. Consider the following:

- Colonialism, Development, and Environmentalism in Africa and Asia: Topics include "deforestation and desertification under colonial rule," "imperialism and conservation," and more.
- Pacific: Empire, Labor, Migration: This course "examines the relationship between migration, race, and empire, with a focus on how US colonialism and imperialism depended on migration and labor of Asian and Pacific peoples."
- Race and Gender in Brazilian Film: "It is the hope that film will offer students an additional cultural context to critically examine the development of [the] nation and national ideologies such as 'the myth of racial democracy.'"
- Gender Cross-Cultural Perspectives: "This course thus pays close attention to issues of power and inequality, including the ways in which Western gender ideals have been imposed on people in other parts of the world."

Course options better poised for comparative study and the principled questions it raises thoroughly investigate a time, place, and culture different from our own without betraying a premature judgment about the "interrelationship" between the objects of study.

- Alexander and Macedonian Kings: A course on "the history of Alexander the Great and of Greek-speaking peoples in the eastern Mediterranean during the fourth through first centuries BCE."
- China to 1800 "explores China's history from its ancient origins to the end of the eighteenth century."
- Trading Places: "This course will investigate and analyze the factors that led to and inhibited development in Chile and Argentina."
- Nuclear Weapons: This course "begins by examining the physical properties of nuclear weapons, and then uses evidence from the Cold War to address the following questions: Why did the United States and Soviet Union build such large nuclear arsenals? What did they plan to do with these weapons? How did nuclear weapons fit into US and Soviet military strategy at various phases of the Cold War?"

SOCIAL ANALYSIS

Roughly two hundred courses offered this fall fulfill the Social Analysis requirement, which provides ample opportunity for students to study the intersection of race, class, and gender. Consider the following:

- Racial Capitalism: Enough said.
- US–Mexican Borderlands: This course takes a "relational ethnic studies approach" in order to understand "how the border was and continues to be contested" and "how [its] origins manifested forms of exclusionary nation-building."
- Gender and Leadership: "Nearly everywhere in the world, gender equity continues to be an aspiration,

rather than a reality, with no end in sight as to when a reasonable degree of parity will ever actually be achieved. . . . What would need to be done to change it?"

- Migrant Nation: "Drawing explicitly on the collective work of the 'hashtag syllabus' movement, this course seeks to contextualize current debates over immigration reform, integration, and citizenship by considering migration from multiple perspectives."

- Gender Issues in Native American Life: This course examines indigenous communities' "responses to misconceptions of tribal gender roles and identities projected upon Native people by the agents and institutions of settler colonialism," including efforts "to deconstruct and decolonize gender categories that are alien to the continuity, integrity, and vitality of their own traditions."

- Dangerous Intersections: An introduction to intersectionality, "interrogat[ing] how power is distributed along and across axes of inequality and privilege."

For students wishing to avoid intersectionality studies, more than twenty-five standard economics courses fulfill the Social Analysis requirement. Other standouts include the two below:

- Adam Smith and Political Economy: "This course focuses on Smith's major ideas through his two important works, *The Theory of Moral Sentiments* and *The Wealth of Nations*, and deals with such topics as the origins and consequences of economic growth, and the role of government in a commercial society."

- Europe in the Age of Wonder: This history course seems to take a refreshing look at what are sometimes dismissed as the Dark Ages, examining the "emergence of early nation states," "expansion of trade," and "advances in scientific thinking" that occurred during a time when "society, economics, politics, and culture were guided by a sense of wonder."

Dartmouth College

QUANTITATIVE AND DEDUCTIVE SCIENCE

More than fifty courses offered this fall fulfill the Quantitative and Deductive Science requirement, all of them serious math-based courses, upholding Dartmouth's mandate that "students must pass a course in mathematics, in mathematical statistics, or in symbolic logic, the underpinning of mathematical reasoning." Based on the number of sections offered, it seems that the most common and perhaps least challenging way to do so is by taking either Intro. to Calculus or Calculus itself, though these courses still look rigorous. Outside of the Mathematics Department, dozens of solid options in computer science and statistics also fulfill the requirement.

NATURAL AND PHYSICAL SCIENCE

Students must take two Natural and Physical Science courses, and either one of these two courses or a Technology or Applied Science course must "provide a laboratory, experimental, or field component as an integral part of its structure." More than seventy-five courses offered this fall fulfill the requirement, and all require the study of an actual science, ranging from astronomy to psychology and including ample options in biology, chemistry, earth sciences, and physics.

TECHNOLOGY OR APPLIED SCIENCE

More than sixty-five courses offered this fall fulfill the Technology or Applied Science requirement, and almost all seem to "address the principles underlying technology or applied science, rather than just making use of technology." Once again, this distributive requirement maintains high standards, refusing to offer students an easy way out of taking a course in an engineering or computer science-related field.

One possible exception, however, is an English course on gaming, Digital Game Studies, which focuses on digital gaming's history and impact on culture, rather than the applied science that makes digital gaming possible.

WESTERN CULTURE (WC)

Explaining that the "disciplines of the Arts and Sciences as they are studied at Dartmouth developed in these [Western] cultures, as did the institution of the liberal arts college itself," Dartmouth requires students to take "at least one course with a focus on the cultures of the West." Many of the roughly one hundred courses offered this fall to fulfill the Western Culture requirement heed the spirit of the catalogue description, offering course topics on the major works and events of Western civilization. Unfortunately, however, more than a few do not.

Some courses appear to have nabbed the "WC" designation by featuring topics on contemporary American or European society, for example, rather than on the "classical Judeo-Christian and Greco-Roman Mediterranean" culture that has shaped Europe and America. Examples of these kinds of misfits include:

- Contemporary Germany: "Society and culture in contemporary Germany."
- Politics of Climate Change: "Drawing upon research from political science, communications, and psychology, this class investigates the public's climate beliefs, attitudes, and behaviors."
- Contemporary Music III: "The contemporary music laboratory will read through and study works appropriate to the participants' skill level."
- US Television History: "The history of television as an emerging technology; its dynamic interaction with government, private industry, and audiences; and its impact on

society and culture."

Other courses appear to have nabbed the WC designation simply by teaching a field or discipline that developed within the West. Examples include:

- Introduction to Film
- Introduction to Public Policy Research
- Introductory Sociology
- Election Polling: A statistics course that does not "focus on the cultures of the West," as the Dartmouth catalogue prescribes.
- Social Movements: "This course examines why and when social movements come about, the organizations and strategies they adopt, and the circumstances in which they are most impactful."
- Political Communication: "This seminar provides an overview of research in political communication with special reference to work on the impact of the mass media on public opinion and voting behavior."
- Sonic Arts II: In this "upper-level sonic arts studio course . . . [s]tudents will expand their technical and creative capacity with Ableton Live and be introduced to software tools for sound synthesis and generative music."
- Organizations in Society: "In this course, we will learn about the structure, internal processes, and environ-ments of different forms of organization."

Of course, no education in Western cultures is complete without a course on fascism. How to Be a Fascist explores questions essential to understanding the cultures of the West, such as, "How do people become fascists? How do they rise to power? Why did people support fascism?"

Many of the worthwhile courses for this require-ment have already been highlighted in previous sections. Among those not yet mentioned, here are some standouts:

- Readings in Greek Prose and Poetry: An intermediate Greek language course with texts "typically including selections from Plato and/or Euripides."
- The Great War and the Transformation of Europe: This course "explores how the First World War redefined warfare, destroyed empires, and profoundly altered the political, social, and cultural landscapes of Europe."
- Dante: *The Divine Comedy*: Taught in English, this course focuses on Dante's *La Vita Nuova* and *Inferno*.
- Society, Culture, and Politics in Spain: "This course studies socio-political events in the Iberian Peninsula that have shaped the contemporary configuration of society in Spain."
- Theatre and Society I: "This course explores selected examples of world performance during the classical and medieval periods in Western Europe and Eastern Asia," with readings including plays by Aeschylus, Sophocles, Euripides, Aristophanes, Seneca, Plautus, Terence, and Zeami.
- Introduction to Classical Archaeology: "This course addresses the basic methods and principles of Classical archaeology through a survey of the sites and artifacts of Greco-Roman antiquity."
- Topics in Latin: Landscape: For this course on Latin literary culture, readings include "a mixture of poetry and prose taken from a variety of authors including Catullus, Cicero, Tibullus, Ovid, Pliny, Martial, and Juvenal."

NON-WESTERN CULTURES

Dartmouth expects its Non-Western Culture requirement to equip students with "knowledge of non-Western peoples, cultures, and histories" as a "practical necessity as well as a form of intellectual enrichment." Indeed, non-Western histories and cultures can provide a wealth of intellectual enrichment, as courses offered on ancient civilizations in Japan, China, and the Middle East demonstrate. Unfortunately, however, many of the almost one hundred courses offered this fall to fulfill the Non-Western Cultures requirement focus not on the cultures but on the alleged oppression of non-Western peoples. Consider the following:

- Rasta and Rastafari: Learn how "Rastafari has offered, cloaked in revolutionary black hermeneutics, some of the sharpest critiques against European imperialism and exploitation."
- Women, Religion, and Social Change in Africa: Central course questions include, "What are the different antecedents and circumstances in which women exercise or are denied agency, leadership, power, and happiness in their communities?"
- Francophone Literature/Culture: This course on the literature of former French colonies "examines the social, political, and cultural issues it raises: race, colonialism, decolonization, revolution, independence, neo-colonialism, *Négritude*, *Antillanité*, *Créolité*, *écriture féminine*, mimetic desire, cultural hybridity, [and] post-independence government and society."
- Women and Migration: "Through a series of Francophone literary texts and films, this course examines how contemporary female writers, filmmakers, and artists respond to the migration, immigration, and displacement of peoples today."
- Introduction to Latin America and the Caribbean: This course examines the colonial history of selected countries in the region as well as "particular case studies of contemporary life and society to analyze the ongoing problems of ethnicity, inequality, and political repression engendered by the region's colonial past."
- Modern Middle East and North Africa: Topics include "European colonialism," "anti-colonial movements," "debates

over the politics of gender," and "the processes of decolonization and the establishment of post-colonial states."

- Transnational Feminism: "Rooted in intersectionality, justice, praxis, and solidarity, the banner of transnational feminism has assembled scholars and activists from diverse social and geopolitical positions through coalitions across global, regional, national, and local borders, both within and beyond the nation-state."

Among those not yet mentioned, better options include:

- Archaeology of the Middle East: "This course provides an introduction to the civilizations of the ancient Middle East and to the history of archaeological research in this important region."
- Emergence of Modern Japan: "A survey of Japanese history from the mid-nineteenth century to the present."

CULTURE AND IDENTITY (CI)

With so many opportunities to obsess over identity through the other requirements, it is almost surprising to see Culture and Identity receive its own superfluous category. Indeed, all of the roughly fifty courses offered this fall to fulfill the CI requirement also fulfill other distributive requirements. The least academically worthwhile options emphasize identity, while the better options emphasize culture. Among courses not yet mentioned, here are some to avoid:

- Identity Politics from a Global Perspective: Topics include "how identity should be conceptualized and measured; why some forms of identity are activated, mobilized, contested; how identities are represented politically; how racial and ethnic identities intersect with other salient identities; how social diversity and civil society are interrelated; what factors affect the integration of immigrants; and which varieties of democracy enable the flourishing of plural identities."

- Gender Identities and Politics in Africa: "This interdisciplinary course explores the constructions of gender identities in different African socio-cultural contexts."
- Intersections: "Students will investigate the categories sex, gender, sexuality, race, class, citizenship, and ability, how they are socially and historically constructed and in relation to one another."
- Sex, Gender, and Society: "This course investigates basic concepts about sex, gender, and sexuality and considers how these categories intersect with issues of race, class, ethnicity, family, religion, age, and/or national identity."
- Introduction to South Asia: "The course will examine the many identities of South Asia, including regional, religious, caste, national, and gender identities, and explore how these identities have been shaped in contexts of change from ancient times to the present."
- Asian American Literature and Culture: "We will analyze novels, short fiction, poetry, and films by twentieth-century artists . . . against the historical backdrop of imperialism in Asia and the Americas; periods of exclusion and internment; and social movements that coalesce around intersections of race, class, gender, sexuality, and citizenship."

Better options include:

- Introduction to Korean Culture: "This course provides an introduction to Korean culture and history, examining Korea's visual and textual expressions from the premodern age to the twentieth century."
- Beyond Good and Evil: "Borrowing its title from Nietzsche, this course examines some of the most famous and infamous figures—mythological, fictional, and historical—that have profoundly shaped German identity."

- History/Culture of Jews: Modern Period: "This course provides a survey of Jewish history and culture from the European enlightenment to the establishment of the State of Israel."
- Introduction to Italian Culture: "This course introduces students to Italian culture through a representative selection of texts and topics from past to present."

Conclusion

Here's what a Dartmouth slacker could get away with to meet all general education requirements, assuming that the courses were offered and available in the right order, and not considering the possibility of double-counting courses.

FIRST-YEAR WRITING REQUIREMENTS

- Performing Gender
- More-Than-Human Narratives: Posthumanism, Ecocriticism, Animal Studies

LANGUAGE REQUIREMENT

- French

DISTRIBUTIVE REQUIREMENTS

- Music and Social Justice
- Ghosts, Monsters, Psychos
- Video Games and the Meaning of Life
- Race and Gender in Brazilian Film
- Dangerous Intersections
- Racial Capitalism
- Intro. to Calculus
- How the Earth Works (with lab)

- Exploring the Universe
- Digital Gaming Studies

WORLD CULTURE REQUIREMENTS

- Politics of Climate Change
- Transnational Feminism
- Identity Politics from a Global Perspective

A serious Dartmouth student could choose far better:

FIRST-YEAR WRITING REQUIREMENTS

- Global Humanities 1
- Paris in the Nineteenth Century

LANGUAGE REQUIREMENT

- Arabic

DISTRIBUTIVE REQUIREMENTS

- Sacred Architecture of Asia
- *The Tale of Genji*
- Religion of Israel: Hebrew Bible
- Alexander and Macedonian Kings
- Adam Smith and Political Economy
- Europe in the Age of Wonder
- Algorithms
- Cell Structure and Function
- General Chemistry (with lab)
- Introduction to Programming and Computation

WORLD CULTURE REQUIREMENTS

- Dante: *The Divine Comedy*
- Archaeology of the Middle East
- Beyond Good and Evil

COLUMBIA UNIVERSITY

Introduction

C olumbia University's century-strong core curriculum is not, for the most part, a smorgasbord of courses set on a table of distribution requirements. It is "a communal learning experience that cultivates community-wide discourse and deliberate contemplation around seminal works, contemporary issues, and humanity's most enduring questions."

This curriculum "is designed to transcend disciplines. It introduces cornerstone ideas and theories from across literature, philosophy, history, science, and the arts, inviting your curiosity, reflection, and critique, in conversation with others." Indeed, one expectation of the curriculum is induction into an "intimate intellectual community" that develops "deep, enduring friendships." Beyond Columbia, students and alumni "join a greater conversation" linking the generations.

Another expectation is development of "intellectual tools and habits of mind you'll use long after you leave college, enabling you to solve multidimensional problems and find answers to profound questions that might at times seem unanswerable." This connection between intellectual development and goals beyond the academy exemplifies "an approach to thinking and living that seeks to elevate society for all."

The histories of Columbia's core curriculum and the idea of "general education" are worth learning but beyond the scope of this book. To reduce the origins of general education to one complex sentence: Educators created general education programs in reaction to the curricular fragmentations of, on the one hand, the disciplinary specializations built for the German-style research university and, on the other hand, the elective system built for Emersonian, Romantic-era self-discovery. Today's colleges commonly maintain, at least in theory, the tripartite undergraduate model of a core, a major concentration in a discipline, and electives. Columbia does so better than most.

Most colleges offer students a large number of courses to fulfill each core-curriculum requirement. Each disciplinary requirement is in effect a "distribution requirement," stemming from the idea that any course in a subject area is as worthy as any other. A student can take any history course, for example, to fulfill a history requirement, because learning facts is said to be secondary to learning how to think and write historically. Columbia instead declares that particular content in each core subject area is what students should learn.

Columbia's Core and Other Requirements

Columbia undergraduates must take all six core courses, plus several "discipline-specific" courses that function as distribution requirements. In the latter courses, "students learn specific content that conveys ways of knowing and understanding." Students also must complete four semesters' worth of proficiency in a foreign language, plus one year of physical education and a swim test (with or without a swimming course).

This book focuses on students' choices—the education a student may choose in addition to specific course requirements. In other words, this chapter is not an evaluation of the quality of Columbia's syllabi in its core courses. Accordingly, this section merely outlines five of the six required courses with minimal commentary. The chapter then examines the choices offered to fulfill the University Writing requirement and, finally, turns to the remaining requirements—Global Core and Science—in which students may choose courses wisely or poorly. (The foreign language requirement is not elaborated here because it simply teaches a language.) Readers should consider these options in the context of the rest of Columbia's generally well-designed curriculum.

Literature Humanities is not, after all, consistent in its syllabus from one year to the next. Since its syllabus is "ever-evolving," Columbia students today may not be studying many of the same books for this requirement as students did decades ago. The goal, whatever the readings, "is to consider a range of perspectives across time and cultures that can enhance our understanding of the world and foster a deeper sense of empathy, while also developing crucial skills in close reading, critical thinking, writing, and academic discussion through the analysis of literary works." As of July 2024, the most recent published iteration of Literature Humanities—a yearlong course sequence called Masterpieces of Western Literature and Philosophy—includes seventeen authors from Enheduanna (an ancient Sumerian) and Homer to Toni Morrison and the relatively unknown Claudia Rankine, plus *Gilgamesh*, the Hebrew Scriptures, and the Gospels.

Art Humanities develops students' "visual literacy" through "analytical study of a limited number of monuments and artists," including field trips across New York City. The studies in the course, named Masterpieces of Western Art, stretch from the Parthenon to Cordoba and farther west to Andy Warhol and living artist Cindy Sherman. Not counting non-Western works and artists encountered on the field trips, the syllabus indeed focuses on the West.

Music Humanities likewise concentrates on the West; its course is named Masterpieces of Western Music. It stresses listening, studying works in context from the Middle Ages on, and hearing music across the city.

Contemporary Civilization, taught in two courses, "has evolved continuously" over the past 105 years of its existence. After all, most of what was contemporary in 1919 is barely remembered in American culture today. Faculty revise the syllabus every three years. The requirement's goal today is to introduce "a range of issues concerning the kinds of communities—political, social, moral, and religious—that human beings construct, and the values that inform and define such communities."

Yet the fall course has, on paper, nothing contemporary in it. Instead, students will find an outstanding array of works beginning with Plato's *Republic* and the Bible's Exodus and surveying highlights up through the usual contract theorists' works by Locke, Hobbes, and Rousseau. There are nods to colonialism in the Conquest of the Americas section, but otherwise, instructors have to make the case that classic texts are relevant "to the pressing problems of our world." Such texts are indeed relevant to every age, which is why they are deemed canonical.

The spring course begins similarly—with Adam Smith and Immanuel Kant—but eventually turns to what one would expect the academy today to think of as the key contemporary issues: "race, gender, and sexuality," "anticolonialism," and, inevitably, "climate." Classic texts include much more that is relevant to today than is captured within such contemporary academic fads, so it is an intellectual and civilizational mistake to treat Contemporary Civilization as eventuating primarily in these topics. The final section of the course is called "Climate and Futures," since contemporary culture is apparently not enough and students also must study the future.

Frontiers of Science intends to "engage students in the process of discovery by exploring topics at the forefront of science and to inculcate or reinforce the specific habits of mind that inform a scientific perspective on the world." Students hear a weekly lecture from a Columbia scientist, then participate in seminars led by postdoctoral students in which they "discuss the lecture and its associated readings" and "debate the implications of the most recent scientific discoveries."

UNIVERSITY WRITING

As at most universities, Columbia's requirement in academic writing involves a wide variety of options. Each category of sections has its own theme, and the themes change over time. From this point of view, the University Writing requirement is less like the other five core courses and more like the distribution requirements. Ten themed choices were available as of July 2024.

Syllabi for these courses are not readily available, but about five years ago the Columbia *Spectator* provided helpful—while disappointing—details about the 2019 offerings. Like so many other universities, Columbia has made its writing requirement a hotbed of progressive posturing.

Three choices that seem not to teach critical thinking or writing but take major premises for granted—and therefore should not be chosen—are:

- Readings in Gender and Sexuality: "What is the relationship between sex, gender, and sexuality? How does gender connect with race, class, disability, and other forms of identity? At what moments do our expressions of our body, gender, and sexuality become a mode of resistance?" Readings from 2019 included such important issues as "The Best $6,250 I Ever Spent: Top Surgery" (Ortberg, who had her breasts removed) and "Women Deserve Orgasm Equality" (Valenti).
- Readings in Climate Humanities: This course takes as given that "climate" is an "existential issue" and that, therefore, it is appropriate to have a course "affirming the relevance of voices that range from experts and activists in organizations like Columbia's Earth Institute to artists, academics, and citizens." The course is "guided by capacious and urgent [and question-begging] questions, such as: What does it mean to live in the Anthropocene? What dynamics of power, both social and material, shape our approaches to the climate crisis?" It's unclear how well this course tolerates those who critically challenge the apparent certainties that Columbia teaches here.
- Readings in Race and Ethnicity: This course clearly displays its edge and outlook in ways inconsistent with a critical academic approach to contemporary issues. Students should skip it. Those who don't will "read and write essays that engage urgent conversations about race and ethnicity to advance social justice. We will study interdisciplinary essays that explore constructs of identity and representation in our everyday lives, as well as essays that interrogate how these constructs operate within systems of oppression and pose strategies for disrupting those systems."

Probably another three to skip are:

- Readings in Urban Studies: This course focuses narrowly on the field of Urban Studies. It engages questions such as, "What problems can and should be addressed through city planning, urban design, and development? How might architecture and urban planning either improve or contribute to social and material problems such as inequality, segregation, and lack of access? In what ways are racial, gender, sexual, class, ability, and other identities shaped by urban life?"
- Readings in Law and Justice: Students "wrestle with core questions of law and justice . . . that have important implications for our lives." Judging by the highlighted 2019 readings, however, the questions and answers alike tend to come from the Left: "Free Feminism Tomorrow" (Ryan Miller), "Beyond the Monochromatic: Suffering and Empathy through the Lens of Intersectionality" (Shannon Sun), and "Themes of 2016: Progressive Parties Have to Address the People's Anger" (Michael Sandel).
- University Writing for International Students: One should wish that this course focuses on something good about America while it helps international students get up to speed on academic vocabulary. That's a vain hope, judging by the 2019 texts listed: "Speaking in Tongues" (Zadie Smith), "Is Cultural Appropriation Always Wrong?" (Parul Sehgal), "Crazy, Salty, Sexy" (Blair Pfander), and "The Case for Reparations" (Ta-Nehisi Coates).

That leaves four options:

- Contemporary Essays ("unthemed"): Example texts from 2019 are not promising: "Brainy or Busty? Both. Sexuality and Intelligence in BBC's *Sherlock*" (Emily Man), and "Fashion's Latest Trend: Pushing the Boundaries of Beauty with Intersectional Identities" (Emily Lau).
- Readings in American Studies: This course engages "a

field marked by its diverse approaches to exploring the culture, history, politics, and ideas that make up American identity and the idea of America itself" so as to "wrestle with core questions that have important implications for life in America and beyond." Example texts from 2019 include the great "What to the Slave Is the Fourth of July?" (Frederick Douglass) and "Letter from Birmingham Jail" (Martin Luther King, Jr.) but also the unnecessarily apocalyptic and melodramatic "American Extremism Has Always Flowed from the Border" (Greg Grandin, writing in *Boston Review* that "the United States stands on the precipice").

- Readings in Film and Performing Arts: "Critical essay-writing as a performative and generative conversation between artists, critics, and audiences." This theme examines "critical essays about a particular artistic medium . . . that interrogate the aesthetic, political, and philosophical stakes of critical reading and writing" and includes "field trips to artistic happenings and workshops with critical writers from Columbia's faculty and beyond."

- Readings in Medical Humanities: Medicine-related texts in "biomedical ethics, medical anthropology, journalism, and literary criticism." Example texts in 2019 included, sadly, "Born a Womyn?: Lisa Vogel's Paradigm for Transgender Exclusion" and "Beyond 'That's Not Funny': Reading Into How We Read a Prison Rape Joke," both by Nadia Khayrallah.

Unfortunately, the contents of the courses that fulfill Columbia's writing requirement do not match up to the rest of the core.

GLOBAL CORE

While Columbia's core focuses primarily on the Western canon, the Global Core options intentionally broaden students' options beyond the West. Students must choose two out of about three hundred choices (not all of which are taught each year).

Students can choose well. For example, there's a masterpieces course that focuses on Indian art and architecture. There's African civilization or Latin American civilization or East Asian civilization with a focus on China, Korea, Japan, or Tibet. There's Egypt, Plato vs. Confucius, Mediterranean humanities (which hardly breaks free of the Western canon, however), or Islamic civilization. There's Buddhism, Judaism, or Hinduism. And many, many more.

Or students can choose poorly. Fortunately, the list of poor choices is short; quality control is generally good. The most notorious use a postcolonial lens. The most notable are:

- Decolonizing the Arabian Nights, which "resituates its advent and vogue in specific cultural contexts that closely relate to the rise of the bourgeoisie and the colonial enterprise."
- Blackness and Frenchness: A Radical Genealogy, which wonders, "How have Black radicals embraced the French language and, at times, Frenchness without espousing France's dominance and its doctrines of assimilation?" The course uses "an intra-imperial and inter-imperial lens."
- *Game of Thrones*: On Epics and Empires, which tries to "examine the main themes and overall arch" of the series "into wider mythic, heroic, and transhistorical dimensions of our contemporary history."
- Berlin/Istanbul: Migration, Culture, Values, a quite narrow course taught in German, which focuses on "the Turkish minority living in Germany today." This could be a good course but not for this core requirement.
- London in Postcolonial Fiction, which "will consider

London as a postcolonial metropolis and former seat of empire and the transatlantic slave trade" and is taught at Queen Mary University through the Columbia in London program.

- Black Paris, taught in Paris, which teaches the "lesser-known face of Paris linked to its colonial past."

SCIENCE BEYOND THE "FRONTIERS" COURSE

Columbia students must take one Science B course and one Science C course. Columbia helpfully puts an asterisk next to courses designed for non-science majors. The easy ones in astronomy look embarrassingly simple. After all, tongue in cheek, the Universal Timekeeper course states that its goal "is to illustrate—and perhaps even inculcate—quantitative and scientific reasoning skills." In Biodiversity, "no previous knowledge of science or mathematics is assumed." And Columbia truly has a course titled Physics for Poets.

Most of the science courses are regular, science-based courses. But a student who prefers activism to science would take Global Warming for Global Leaders to increase their "confidence and ability to engage in public discourse on the subject of climate change, climate change solutions, and public policy concerning our collective future." No development of the skepticism of the scientist is apparent in this course.

Conclusion

There is no room for slackers at Columbia. Most of the core curriculum is not just required but also, at least on paper, academically rich and rigorous. Columbia Lions can, however, take advantage of the writing requirement and the Global Core options to find courses that do not live up to Columbia's otherwise high standards, and climate activists can even forgo a lot of science and scientific method in their science requirements by taking the global warming courses. Yet, compared to the rest of the Ivy League, the college curriculum at Columbia University stands out.

How, then, could Columbia be the site of such antisemitism and lawlessness following the Hamas attack in Fall 2023? Is the core failing to teach basic ethics? It is important to understand that the enrollment of Columbia College is less than five thousand out of a total enrollment of thirty-six thousand. There are roughly five thousand more undergraduates in engineering or in General Studies, and there are another twenty-six thousand graduate students. But twenty thousand of Columbia University's students are international students. (Columbia counts graduates who are engaged in post-graduation job training as part of this total.) Half of them are from China. With such a large student body, it takes just a small proportion of international graduate students, plus some New York–area residents, to cause considerable chaos.

It's not the undergraduate core that should be blamed for the poor education and behavior of Columbia students; blame instead the offices and departments responsible for graduate admissions for failing to filter out miscreants who received a bad undergraduate education somewhere else.

BROWN UNIVERSITY

The College at Brown University boasts an "Open Curriculum" rather than general education requirements as the key to a strong liberal arts education. While recognizing that a liberal arts education entails "a breadth of knowledge across multiple academic fields of study," Brown nevertheless leaves it up to the student to acquire this breadth as the "architect of [his or her] own educational experience."

Central to the 1969 adoption of the Open Curriculum, according to accounts of its history, was the idea that a strict separation of academic disciplines was not conducive to a liberal arts education. To foster interdisciplinary learning, then, the Open Curriculum removed potential obstacles to stepping outside of students' academic comfort zones. Brown shed distributive requirements and GPAs, permitting any course to be taken pass/fail, and replacing "majors" with "concentrations"—"broad, interdisciplinary fields of study."

In keeping with these commitments, Brown imposes only four degree requirements on undergraduates:

1. Complete at least thirty courses.
2. Complete one of eighty concentrations, or create your own with approval of the College Curriculum Council.

3. Complete the college's two-part writing requirement.
4. Complete eight full-time semesters at Brown, four of which must be in residence.

Although Brown's Open Curriculum may have seemed radical at the time of its adoption, its openness no longer distinguishes it very far beyond the undergraduate curricula of other Ivy League universities. With the exception of Columbia, the Ivies' distributional "requirements" include so many options as to approach an "open" curriculum. Nor do Brown's interdisciplinary ideals necessarily set it apart, since many of the concentrations meant to exemplify these ideals—from Africana Studies to South Asian Studies—seem instead to reinforce specialization, albeit in an identity group rather than a discipline, studies that also are now common across the Ivies. Indeed, Brown's commitment to oppression studies is underlined by its "strong encouragement" to first-year students to enroll in either a first-year seminar or a course on "Race, Power, and Privilege."

Still, the courses available to fulfill Brown's writing requirement suggest that a liberal arts education is still within reach for the student who knows what to look for. As with our writeups on other universities, the sections below focus on Brown's one requirement—the writing courses—as well as its "Race, Power, and Privilege" push.

WRITING

To ensure that undergraduates work on their writing skills throughout their college career, Brown implements a two-part writing requirement: at least one writing-designated course during their first four semesters at Brown, and at least one during their second four semesters. Writing-designated courses include all English,

Literary Arts, and Comparative Literature courses, in addition to courses outside of those disciplines that merit the "writing" designation. Biology, German Studies, and Math concentrators "may submit writing completed in the concentration" to satisfy the second part of the writing requirement.

More than 250 courses offered this fall fulfill Brown's writing requirement. Some of the least worthwhile, from a liberal arts perspective, include:

- Seven Hours and Fifty-Five Minutes: Sex, Work, and Migration in Global Contexts: With a title derived from Thailand's first "sex worker rights" organization, this course examines "forms of work that are inflected by race, gender, class, nation, and ability."
- Black to the Future: Race as Science Fiction: "How does Black science fiction in both literary and visual form, teach us how to see and read blackness otherwise?"
- Producing the Body: The Body as Performance of Power, Violence, and Possibility: "This course will deeply consider what it means to be (in)human, erotic reconfigurations of being, and fugitive practice."
- Making Music American: Critical Heritage Studies: "We will particularly attend to public performance contexts, including music festivals, club dancefloors, and live-streaming/archived online performances."
- Writing and Resistance in Indigenous America (1500–1700): This class examines "the mechanisms of Indigenous resistance within the developing structures of colonialism: race, religion, geography, and gender."
- Race, Crime, and Punishment in America: Topics include "racial disparities in punishment," "policing and race relations in American cities," and the "stereotypes and economics of crime."
- Critical Black Masculinities and Education: "This course unpacks the various ways that masc-identifying people

leverage, experience, and correct patriarchy as a destructive force," focusing on "the educational life-worlds of Black male, men, and/or masc-identifying people in institutions of colleges and universities, prisons, community initiatives, and even healthcare systems."

- What Is Work? Race, Gender, and Sexuality at Work: "How is work differently configured along lines of race, gender, sexuality, class, and dis/ability?"
- Early American Lives: This seventeenth- to nineteenth-century American history course focuses on "studies of a female Mohawk, a renegade New England colonist, an enslaved African American woman who escaped from George Washington, a lesbian couple, a forgotten nineteenth-century celebrity, and a Civil War spy."
- Understanding the Palestinians: "The course covers the modern period (1750 to the present) and engages larger themes of capitalist transformation, imperialism, settler-colonialism, nationalism, and indigeneity."
- Sex, Power, and God: A Medieval Perspective: "Cross-dressing knights, virgin saints, homophobic priests, and mystics who speak in the language of erotic desire are but some of the medieval people considered in this seminar."
- American Education Policy in Historical and Comparative Perspective: Topics include "the ways in which 'school choice' has intersected in practice and in theory with segregation, integration, and debates over mechanisms to improve school quality."
- The (Racial) Politics of National Culture: "We will explore the nexus between national culture, identity, citizenship, and whiteness in Western nations with a focus on France, the US, and possibly others."
- How Can Activists Change the World? The Dynamics of Power and Resistance: The title pretty much says it all.
- *Bella Ciao*: Resistances in Contemporary Italian Culture: This course examines "artistic expressions of resistance

performed against different forms of power (nationalism, the colonial state, the patriarchal family, the Mafia,
the Church, police violence)."

- Text/Media/Culture: Theories of Modern Culture and
  Media: "We will read semiotic theory, critical race studies,
  feminist, post-colonial, queer, and political theory, and examine concepts such as textuality, visuality, and networks."

Other misfits include computer science and lab science
courses that do not appear to focus on writing.

The serious liberal arts student, on the other hand, has
good options to choose from, including:

- Archaeologies of the Greek Past: "This course will
  explore the material world of ancient Greece, from the
  monumental (the Parthenon) to the mundane (waste
  management), and everything in between."
- The Idea of Self: Readings draw from Sappho, Pindar,
  Catullus, Horace, Augustine, and Fortunatus "to gauge
  the peculiar nature of what [literary] knowledge tells us
  about experience and the ways in which expressions of
  selfhood abide or are changed over time."
- Roman History II: The Roman Empire and Its Impact:
  Topics include the "expansion, administration, and Roman-
  ization of the empire," the "struggle between paganism and
  Christianity," and the "end of the Empire in the West."
- Murder Ink: Narratives of Crime, Discovery, and Identity: This course on the narrative of detection offers a
  cultural feast for the mind, with readings of *Oedipus Rex*,
  Hamlet, and Poe's "The Murders in the Rue Morgue," as
  well as film viewings of Preminger's *Laura* (1944) and
  Hitchcock's *Vertigo* (1958).
- The Pursuit of Happiness: "This course will study the
  emergence of the modern concept of happiness from the
  ancient ideal of the 'good life' to the notion of 'pursuit
  of happiness' as an 'inalienable right.'" Readings draw

from thinkers including Montesquieu, Johnson, Voltaire, and Rousseau, as well as political texts in the American, French, and Haitian traditions.

- Islands in the Western Imaginary: Paradise, Periphery, Prison: This course examines the meaning of the island in Western literature. "Authors may include Homer, Plato, Marco Polo, Mandeville, Darwin, Defoe, Tournier, Kincaid, Kafka, Durrell, [or] Seferis."
- Shakespeare: The greatest hits.
- Tolkien and the Renaissance: "This course explores the work of J. R. R. Tolkien alongside Renaissance forbears such as Shakespeare, Spenser, Milton, and others."
- Kafka's Writing: "This course provides an introduction to Kafka's stories, novels, journal entries, and letters, with a focus on his complicated, tortured relationship to the idea and practice of writing."
- Friendship in the Ancient World: "How have ancient societies understood friendship, and how do ancient ideas about friendship differ from or resemble those of contemporary Westerners?" Course texts include Homer's *Iliad*, the Book of Ruth, and Aristotle's *Nicomachean Ethics*.

Race, Power, and Privilege, and First-Year Seminar

Although writing is the only enforced substantive requirement outside of concentration requirements, Brown strongly encourages first-year students to take a Race, Power, and Privilege course or First-Year Seminar. The former courses "examine issues of structural inequality, racial formations, and/or disparities and systems of power within a complex, pluralistic world," while the latter "aim to promote close interaction between faculty and students in a small setting that encourages pedagogical innovation and community-building."

RACE, POWER, AND PRIVILEGE

Roughly eighty courses offered this fall carry the Race, Power, and Privilege designation. Standouts include:

- Race and Gender in the Scientific Community: "This course examines the (1) disparities in representation in the scientific community, (2) issues facing different groups in the sciences, and (3) paths towards a more inclusive scientific environment."
- Myriad Mediterraneans: Archaeology, Representation, and Decolonization: "Can archaeology contribute to current debates about decolonization? Conversely, can contemporary debates about indigenous ways of being shine a fresh light on ancient evidence?"
- Teaching LGBTQIA History: "What could a high-school US history class look, sound, and feel like when taught through the experiences of LGBTQIA people and communities?"
- Cultivating STEM Identities: Teaching for Equity in the Math and Science Classrooms: "This course will explore how educational experiences and beliefs about identity and power influence how we learn and teach mathematics and science."
- Queer Asias: "This seminar investigates the politics of non-normative gender and sexuality transnationally across contexts like Indonesia, Korea, the Philippines, and Pakistan."
- The Politics of Contemporary Black Popular Music: "Overall, this course investigates the aesthetic, political, cultural, and economic dimensions of black popular music, paying particular attention to questions of gender, sexuality, class, nation, language, and technology."
- Pathology to Power: Disability, Health, and Community: "This course offers a comprehensive view of health and community concerns experienced by people with disabilities."

- Monuments, Citizenship, and Belonging: "Struggles over racist monuments—from defacement, to unsanctioned removal by protesters, to laws passed to 'protect' statues—raise important questions about the political impact of commemoration."

FIRST-YEAR SEMINAR

Almost fifty courses offered this fall are First-Year Seminars, with most also carrying the "writing" or "Race, Power, and Privilege" designation. Lowlights include:

- Seven Hours and Fifty-Five Minutes: Sex, Work, and Migration in Global Contexts
- Myriad Mediterraneans: Archaeology, Representation and Decolonization
- What is Work? Race, Gender, and Sexuality at Work
- *Bella Ciao*: Resistances in Contemporary Italian Culture

Highlights include:

- The Pursuit of Happiness
- Islands in the Western Imaginary: Paradise, Periphery, Prison
- Friendship in the Ancient World

Our Recommendations

Brown's Open Curriculum lets students avoid both the best and the worst of the university's courses. Students should resist pressure to take a Race, Power, and Privilege course. Take Friendship in the Ancient World as a first-year seminar, engage with Shakespeare and Kafka to meet the writing requirement, and choose a concentration wisely.

CONCLUSION:
SLACKERS OR STRIVERS?

The name of an Ivy League institution on a resume or diploma reveals very little about a graduate's academic preparation. With the partial exception of Columbia, all that an observer should infer is that the graduate had been admitted, did not fail a specified number of courses, fulfilled other requirements (for the major, electives, and sometimes swimming), and showed good enough behavior over about four years that he or she was not expelled.

Not just higher education in general, but elite higher education in particular, has lost much of its shine in recent years. Consider the Ivies' admissions, encampment, and plagiarism scandals. Consider their perennially poor records on free speech and campus culture regarding toleration. Consider their faculty activism. Consider their ideological monocultures. Consider their extreme sticker prices.

And, now, consider the drivel that these institutions offer in the name of higher education. An undergraduate can build a great academic experience at any of the institutions, but most students don't. Outside the hard sciences, the faculty in each case offers so many weak, fragmented, overspecialized, question-begging, frivolous, self-indulgent courses that serious students need serious advice separating the sheep from the goats, the wheat from the chaff.

INDEX

Abelard, Peter, 83
#AbolishPolice, 82
acting, 16, 62
activism, 2, 3, 22–23, 32,
    48, 52, 65, 71, 74, 78, 94,
    114, 118–19, 130, 144, 145,
    150, 155; climate, 50
Aeschylus, 38, 39, 128
aesthetics, 86, 87, 122
Africa, 129, 131
agriculture, 59
AI (artificial intelligence),
    33, 115
Akkadian language, 41
alchemy, 37
Alexander the Great, 54,
    59, 123, 133
algebra, 51, 101
algorithms, 13, 33, 84,
    102, 133
American Council of
    Trustees and Alumni, 2

American History, 2, 22,
    58, 59, 70, 95, 150; Amer-
    ican Economic History,
    34, 43, 45
American Studies, 25–6
Anime, 71, 86, 119
Anselm, 83
anthropology, 19, 21, 52,
    96, 97, 105, 142
anti-Semitism, 37, 145
Aquinas, Thomas, 35, 83
Arabian Nights, 143
Arabic language, 12, 92,
    116, 133
archaeology, 19, 39, 54, 58,
    75, 80, 128, 130, 134, 151,
    153, 154
architecture, 24, 55, 62, 115,
    119, 133, 141, 143
Argentina, 123
Arendt, Hannah, 16, 35
Aristophanes, 15, 128

Index

Aristotle, 10, 35, 38, 39, 97, 122; *Nicomachean Ethics*, 152

art, 15, 23, 25, 37, 53, 54, 60, 71, 97, 117, 118–19, 143; queer; 55

art history, 24, 115, 118–19, 138

Asian Americans, 17, 40, 42, 44, 114, 131

Asian Studies, 8

astrology, 37

astronomy, 14, 41, 101, 125, 144

astrophysics, 64

Athens, Greece, 138, 151

Augustine, 35, 39, 121, 151

autism, 112

Aztecs, 74

Bacon, Francis, 83

Bad Bunny, 10, 94

Balibar, Étienne, 16

ballet, 100

Barbie, 8

Beauvoir, Simone de, 35

Beowulf, 15

Berlin, Germany, 143

Beyoncé, 10, 14, 37

Bible, the, 38, 72, 121, 133, 137, 138

Big Data, 84

biochemistry, 13, 27, 104

biology, 8, 13, 26–27, 40, 42, 45, 52, 62–63, 65, 66, 68, 75, 81, 102, 114, 125, 149

Black Elk, 39

#BlackLivesMatter, 33

Blackness, 18, 23, 32, 44, 143, 149

botany, 91

Bradstreet, Anne, 15

Brazil, 114, 119, 122, 132

British Empire, 99

Brown University, 1, 3, 147–54

Buddhism, 14, 119, 143

Burke, Edmund, 35

Byzantine Empire, 99

Caesar, 10

calculus, 29, 44, 51, 102, 125, 132

Camp Fire Girls, 8

capitalism, 15, 18, 19, 20, 21, 23, 24, 42, 43, 83, 93, 123, 132, 150

Cardi B, 3, 4, 9, 94

Caribbean, 21, 129

cars, driverless, 105

Catullus, 128, 151

Cayuga language, 21

Cervantes, Miguel de, 38, 113

Charlottesville, Virginia, 14

Chaucer, Geoffrey, 15, 24, 38, 43

Chekhov, Anton, 113

chemistry, 26, 41, 42, 62,

63–64, 65, 75, 101, 102,
109, 125, 133; organic, 81
Chile, 123
China, 22, 24, 26, 32, 75,
97, 123, 129, 143, 145
Cicero, 10, 128
citizenship, global, 12, 21
civics, 69, 72, 86, 87
civil disobedience, 16, 82
class, 9, 19, 20, 23, 43, 57,
115, 118, 123, 131, 140,
141, 149
Cleopatra, 10, 29
climate change, 21, 27, 50,
56, 57, 73, 75, 76, 81, 82,
85, 86, 103, 104, 105, 108,
113–14, 126, 133, 144
Coates, Ta-Nehisi, 93, 141
cognitive science, 51
Cold War, 24, 37, 61,
82, 123
colonialism, 8, 16, 17, 18, 19,
23, 37, 40, 41, 42, 43, 53,
82, 93, 105, 114, 117, 118,
122, 129, 138, 149; settler,
81, 100, 120, 124
Columbia University, 1, 2,
3, 11, 135–45, 148, 155
comedy, 100
comic books, 9, 71, 100
communication, an-
imal, 26
communication, polit-
ical, 127
computer science, 41, 51,

81, 84, 102, 125, 133, 151
Confucianism, 119
conservatism, 34
conspiracy theories, 37,
40, 78, 91
Constant, Benjamin, 9
constitutional interpretation, 106
cooking, 75
Cordoba, Spain, 138
Cornell University, 1, 5–29,
94; College of Arts and
Sciences (CAS), 6–7
costume, 23, 28
country music, 37
Critical Native American
and Indigenous Studies
(NAIS), 93, 97
critical race studies, 53,
114, 151
cross-cultural analysis,
53–54, 66
Crucible, The, 8
Crusades, the, 59, 99
cults, 98
Cyrus, Miley, 10

dance, 42, 99, 100
Dante Alighieri, 3, 4, 10,
29, 38, 128, 134
Daoism, 119
Dartmouth College,
1, 111–34
Darwin, Charles, 38, 152
data science, 13, 27, 41, 45,

65, 67, 68, 69, 70, 84, 86, 87, 109
dating, 49
Davis, Angela, 9, 99, 108
deafness, 18
Declaration of Independence, 8
decolonization, 16, 36, 43, 53, 61, 66, 93, 96, 100, 105, 114, 130, 143, 153, 154
Defoe, Daniel, 152
Delvey, Anna, 91
democracy, 15, 33, 34, 35, 38, 39, 59, 73, 98, 122, 131
Derrida, Jacques, 121
Descartes, René, 38, 83
dinosaurs, 32
disability, 14, 18, 23, 25, 28, 43, 49, 91, 92–93, 97, 108, 140, 153
Disney films, 2
diversity, cultural, 54–56, 66, 67
Dostoevsky, Fyodor, 120
Douglass, Frederick, 39, 142
drama, ancient, 60, 68
drinking, 37
Du Bois, W. E. B., 9, 35
Durkheim, Emile, 35
Durrell, Lawrence, 152

earth sciences, 41, 125
Earth Systems Science, 64
ecology, 8, 17, 21, 27, 62, 63, 118
econometrics, 26, 52, 67, 84
economics, 25, 26, 34, 40, 41, 42, 57, 63, 84, 87, 91, 102, 106, 109, 124, 149
ecosocialism, 96, 114
ecosystems, 8, 13, 81, 87, 103, 108
Egypt, 22, 143
Einstein, Albert, 113
Eliot, T. S., 38
Elliott, Missy, 10
Emerson, Ralph, 35, 136
engineering, 3, 16, 41, 65, 79, 81, 87, 88, 89, 103, 104, 105, 108, 109, 125, 145; chemical and biochemical, 104; environmental, 101
Enheduanna, 137
environmental justice, 21, 28, 57, 96
epics, 43, 60, 101, 143
epistemology, 89, 94–95, 107, 109
ethics, 8, 12, 15–17, 34, 37, 65, 69, 72–74, 87, 96, 101, 105, 114, 145; biomedical, 142; of climate change, 73, 86; reproductive, 121–22
ethnography, 93, 96, 105
Euripides, 39, 120, 128
evolution, 63, 76

exceptionalism, American, 20, 32, 44
existentialism, 72, 87, 100
exoplanets, 65, 101
Exorcist, The (film), 79

family, 34, 49, 57, 93, 131, 151
Fanon, Frantz, 100, 108
fascism, 83, 127
Faust, 120
femininity, 8
feminism, 9, 14, 28, 36, 55, 71, 97, 113, 114, 141; Black, 20, 93; early American, 115; post-feminism, 10; transnational, 130, 133
film studies, 14, 22, 37, 60, 77, 78, 79, 94, 95, 96, 99, 100, 115, 118–19, 122, 142
First World War, 128
Fortunatus, 151
Foundation for Individual Rights and Expression (FIRE), 73
Frankenstein (novel), 42, 90
Frankfurt School, 15
Franklin, Benjamin, 15
free speech, 78, 87
French language, 11, 19, 20, 28, 44, 86, 92, 108, 121, 132, 143, 152
French Revolution, 16
Freud, Sigmund, 16
Friedkin, William, 79

Galilei, Galileo, 38
"Game of Thrones," 143
gaming. *See* videogames
Gandhi, Mahatma, 39
gaslighting, 91
gender, 8, 9, 10, 12, 14, 19, 20, 23, 28, 36, 40, 41, 42, 43, 49, 52, 54, 55, 61, 62, 66, 76, 80, 90, 91, 93–94, 96, 98, 105, 112, 113, 115, 118, 119, 121, 122, 123, 124, 131, 132, 139, 140, 141, 149, 150, 153, 154; and mental health, 77–78; politics of, 130; psychology of, 34, 53; sociology of, 57
Gender Studies, 18, 38, 106
genetics, 13, 62; genetic engineering, 80
Genji, Tale of, 120, 133
George, Robert P., 106
German language, 11, 19, 77, 92, 120, 143, 149
Germany, 8, 59, 126, 131, 136
Gilgamesh, Epic of, 58, 94, 137
globalization, 18, 24, 70, 105
Goethe, Johann Wolfgang von, 38, 120
Gothic literature, 20
Gracchi, the, 10, 29
graduate programs, 145
Grandin, Greg, 142

Greece, ancient, 15, 59, 60,
    72, 80, 119, 151, 123, 151
Greek, Ancient, 12, 14–15,
    29, 45, 59, 67, 72, 87, 88,
    92, 94, 109, 120, 128
Greek Myth, 8, 72
grievance, 8
guns, 74, 86

Haiti, 152
Haitian Revolution, 16
Halberstam, Jack, 42
Hamilton (musical), 32
Harvard University, 1, 69–
    88; anti-Israel protests at
    (2024), 73; Faculty of Arts
    and Sciences, 79; Paulson
    School of Engineering
    and Applied Sciences, 79
Hawthorne, Nathaniel, 113
Hebrew language, 92
Heidegger, 39
Hellenism, 54, 59, 94
Herodotus, 35, 120
heroes, 72
heteronormativity, 72
heterosexuality, 8, 9
Hinduism, 119, 143
hip-hop, 9
history, 13, 14, 15, 21, 22,
    23, 24, 36, 37, 43, 48, 54,
    58–59, 61, 66, 67, 70, 71,
    74, 78, 80, 92, 94, 98, 99,
    105, 118, 121, 123, 124,
    126, 129, 130, 131, 132,
135, 136, 142, 143, 147;
    "deep", 75, 87; intellectu-
    al, 83, 88; LGBTQIA, 153;
    Roman, 151
Hitchcock, Alfred, 151
HIV/AIDS, 40
Hobbes, Thomas, 35,
    83, 138
Holmes, Elizabeth, 91
Homer, 38, 72, 120, 137,
    152; *Iliad, The*, 39, 94, 152;
    Odyssey, The, 10, 14, 94
homosexuality, 37,
    55, 71, 76
Horace, 151
horror, 120
human rights, 52, 119
humanities, 2, 7, 8, 12, 27,
    28, 29, 35, 36, 44, 45, 48,
    61, 67, 68, 79, 87, 88, 97,
    112, 113, 115, 133, 137, 138,
    140, 142, 143
Hunger Games, The, 8

identity politics, 2, 12, 17,
    20, 26, 32, 49, 53, 56, 93,
    112, 117, 118, 130–31, 140,
    148, 153
immigration, 11, 16, 18, 42,
    56, 115, 124, 129, 131
indigenous peoples, 12, 14,
    17, 18, 20, 32, 42, 59, 93,
    97, 105, 114, 118–19, 120,
    124, 149, 150, 153
Industrial Revolution, 59

inequality, 8, 11, 12, 18, 19, 33, 40, 43, 52, 56, 82, 83, 119, 122, 124, 129, 141, 152
Inquisition, Spanish, 21
interdisciplinarity, 38, 85, 94, 102, 112, 115, 131, 147, 148
international development, 41, 44
intersectionality, 9, 10, 18, 23, 25, 28, 56, 96, 100, 103, 113, 115, 123, 124, 130, 131, 132, 141
investments, 106
Iran, 20, 22
Israel, State of 32, 121, 132
Istanbul, Turkey, 143
Italian language, 77, 92, 101, 109, 132, 150, 154

January 6th 2021, 8, 14, 33, 82
Japan, 71, 97, 100, 120, 129, 130, 143
Japanese language, 77, 92
Jews, 19, 121, 132
Johnson, Samuel, 152
Joyce, James, 120
Judaism, 24
Juvenal, 128

K-Pop, 33, 53
Kafer, Alison, 49
Kafka, Franz, 152, 154
Kant, Immanuel, 35, 38, 138, 154
Kendi, Ibram X., 82
Khayrallah, Nadia, 142
Kincaid, Lawrence, 152
King Jr., Martin Luther, 142
Korea, 54, 97, 131, 143, 153
Korean language, 92

L'Ouverture, Toussaint, 16
land acknowledgements, 9
languages, foreign. See Akkadian language; Arabic language; Cayuga language; French language; German language; Greek, Ancient; Hebrew language; Italian language; Korean language; Latin language; Portuguese language; Russian language; Spanish language; Swahili language, Swedish language; Tigrinya language; Turkish language; Ukrainian language; Urdu language; Zulu language
Latin America, 129, 143
Latin language, 12, 128; medieval, 101
Latinos, 18
Lau, Emily, 141
law (legal), 17, 20, 25, 29, 56, 61–62, 63, 67, 98, 106, 141; anthropology of, 96

Index

Lenape people, 93
liberalism, 9, 18, 34
Lil Nas X, 10
Lincoln, Abraham, 35
linguistics, 12, 41, 51, 95, 98, 101, 109; Northern Iroquoian, 16
literature, 12, 14, 15, 19, 20, 22, 24, 29, 38, 43, 45, 53, 60, 61, 67, 72, 77, 78, 89, 94, 97, 98, 99–101, 108, 109, 114, 115, 117, 119–20, 129, 131, 135, 137, 149, 152
Locke, John, 35, 138
logic, 13, 51, 52, 73, 101, 104, 125
London, England, 21, 27, 28, 143–44
Lorde, Audre, 33
Lucian, 15
Luther, Martin, 83

macroeconomics, 26
Machiavelli, Niccolo, 35, 83, 97
Madonna, 10
magic, 20, 97–98
Man, Emily, 141
Manga, 100
Mann, Thomas, 120
Manne, Kate, 91
Manson murders, 14
Mao Zedong, 24
Maoism, 24
Marlowe, Christopher, 120

Martial, 128
martial arts, 37
Marx, Karl, 9, 16, 35, 112
Marxism, 9, 19, 99
masculinity, 9, 10, 149
mathematics, 7, 27, 41, 63, 81, 101, 125, 144, 153; applied, 80; history of, 102
Maya, 74
Mean Girls (film), 8
mechanics, 29, 64, 68, 81, 104
Medea, 115
Megan Thee Stallion, 9
Mesopotamia, 58
#MeToo, 33
Mexico, 74
Michelet, Jules, 16
microbiology, 26, 29
microeconomics, 26, 29, 45, 67, 106, 108
Middle Ages, 10–11, 17, 24, 73, 98, 101, 109, 124, 128, 138, 150
Middle East, 24, 58, 129, 130, 134
migration, 18, 19, 40, 41, 122, 124, 129, 143, 149, 154
militarism, 33, 114
Mill, J. S., 38–39
Miller, Ryan, 141
Milton, John, 15, 38, 43, 152
Minoans, 80
Moctezuma, 74

Index

Monáe, Janelle, 37
monsters, 60, 67, 120, 132
Montaigne, Michel de,
    83, 121
Montesquieu, 97, 152
More, Thomas, 83
Morocco, 32
Morrison, Toni, 116, 137
Muhammad, 8
museums, 72, 75, 105
music, 9, 21, 41, 51, 60, 94,
    118, 126, 127, 132, 138,
    149; animal, 115; coun-
    try, 37; phonetics of, 64,
    67; pop, 10, 28, 33, 153;
    theory, 103
Myceneans, 80
Myers-Briggs test, 106

Native Americans, 73, 93,
    97, 120, 124
navigation, celestial, 84, 86
Nazism, 59
neoliberalism, 9, 18,
    23, 54, 91
neurodiversity, 112
neuroscience, 63, 64, 104
New York City, 138, 145
Newton, Isaac, 64
Nietzsche, 35, 38, 112,
    121, 131
nuclear weapons, 123

occult, 37
Ockham, William, 83

Old English, 12
ORLAN (artist), 90
Ovid, 128

paganism, 151
Pakistan, 153
Palestinians, 18, 32, 121, 150
Paris, France, 115, 133, 144
Paris Commune, 16
Pascal, Blaise, 121
pedagogy, 26, 152
Pennsylvania, University of
    (Penn), 1, 47-68; School
    of Arts and Sciences, 47
Persia, 54, 59
Petrarch, 83
Petras, Kim, 10
Pfander, Blair, 141
Philippines, the, 153
philosophy, 8, 10, 11, 12, 15,
    20, 34, 38, 39, 41, 43, 45,
    57, 61, 68, 72, 79, 95, 117,
    121, 135, 137, 142; aesthet-
    ics, 119, 122; Ancient
    Greek, 59, 80, 88; early
    modern, 17; feminist
    political, 96, 108; modern
    political, 29
physical education, 5, 28,
    62, 111, 137
physical sciences, 13,
    26-27, 63, 65, 116, 117, 125
physics, 29, 41, 45, 64, 68,
    75, 81, 88, 102, 103, 113,
    125; computational, 65;

for poets, 2, 144; ther-
  mal, 104, 109
Pindar, 151
plagiarism, 155
planetary sciences, 41
Plato, 15, 35, 38, 121, 128,
  138, 143, 152
Plautus, 128
Pliny, 128
Plotinus, 122
Plutarch, 120
poetry, 20, 55; Chinese, 94
political science, 22, 25, 38,
  106, 126
Polo, Marco, 152
pop culture, 86
pop music. *See under* music
pornography, 96
Portuguese language, 92
possession, spiritual, 36
post-feminism. *See under*
  feminism
Posthumanism, 112–13, 132
Powerpuff Girls (television
  show), 8
Preminger, Otto, 151
Princeton University,
  1, 89–109
prisons, 25, 150, 152, 154
probability, 29, 52, 65, 102
pronouns, 93–94, 107
Proust, Marcel, 38
psychiatry, 36, 100
psychoanalysis, 55, 93, 100
psychology, 12, 16, 34, 38,

39, 55, 67, 125, 126
developmental, 17
experimental, 63
moral, 8
psychotherapy, 76, 86, 115
public health, 40, 44
punishment, 33, 149
punk rock, 14, 28

quantitative reasoning, 6,
  7, 13, 25, 31, 32, 40–41,
  44, 45, 47, 51, 52, 66, 67,
  69, 70, 83–85, 86, 87, 89,
  101–102, 108, 109, 117,
  125, 144
quantum mechanics, 104
queer theory, 14, 18, 49, 55,
  62, 151

race, 8, 9, 12, 14, 18, 20, 23,
  33–34, 40, 43, 49, 52, 54,
  56, 59, 61, 62, 66, 74, 75,
  78, 93, 94, 96, 112, 113,
  115, 118, 119, 121, 122, 123,
  129, 131, 132, 139, 140,
  148, 149, 150, 152, 153,
  154. *See also* critical race
  studies
Rancière, Jacques, 16
Rankine, Claudia, 137
Rawls, John, 9, 112
reality TV, 33, 37, 49, 66, 91
religion, 12, 17, 18, 19, 20,
  23, 54, 62, 74, 79, 87, 93,
  95, 97, 98, 117, 118, 121,

129, 131, 133, 138, 149
Renaissance, 152
reparations, 93, 105, 141
rhetoric, 41, 49
Robespierre, Maximi-
    lien, 16
robots, 8
Roman Empire, 10, 54,
    59, 151
Roman Republic, 10, 29,
    98, 109
Rousseau, Jean-Jacques, 16,
    35, 121, 138, 152
Rushmore, Mount, 32
Russian language, 92

Sageyowatha, 15
Sallust, 10
Sandel, Michael, 141
Sappho, 120, 151
Sartre, Jean-Paul, 121
Schiller, Friedrich, 122
science, philosophy of, 34
science fiction, 149
sciences, hard, 5, 12, 13,
    25, 26, 27, 29, 67, 68, 75,
    80, 155
Seferis, Giorgios, 152
Sehgal, Parul, 141
Seneca, 39, 128
Shaftesbury, Lord, 122
Shakespeare, William, 2,
    14, 37, 38, 39, 43, 99, 152,
    154; *Hamlet*, 15, 101, 109;
    Romeo and Juliet, 113

Sherman, Cindy, 138
Shi'ism, 20
Shintoism, 119
shoes, 105, 107
Sign Language, Ameri-
    can, 11, 18
"1619 Project," 32, 82
slavery, 93, 121, 144, 150
Smith, Adam, 35, 124,
    133, 138
Smith, Zadie, 141
Social Contract, 16
social sciences, 2, 7, 13,
    25–26, 31–35, 44, 45, 48,
    52, 54, 61, 67, 68, 79, 81,
    85, 87, 88,
sociology, 56–57, 66,
    117, 127
Sophocles, 38, 39, 112, 128;
    Oedipus Rex, 151
South Africa, 32
South Asia, 18, 60, 131, 140
Southeast Asia, 13–14
Soviet Union, 123
Spain, 19
Spanish language, 22, 77
Spears, Britney, 10
Spenser, Edmund, 152
Spinoza, Baruch, 15, 17
sports, 33, 34, 43, 44, 78
statistics, 25, 27, 41, 52, 102,
    109, 125, 127
STEM, 36, 40, 44, 153
Stewart, Kristen, 37
storytelling, 8, 62, 67, 99

Index

Stryker, Susan, 42
Styles, Harry, 10
Sun, Shannon, 141
Supreme Court, US, 17, 33
Swahili language, 92
Swedish language, 77
swimming, 5, 28, 111,
 137, 155

television, 8, 91, 100, 126
Terence, 128
Teresa of Avila, 39
Thailand, 149
Thanksgiving, 32
theology, 17, 72
Thucydides, 35, 38, 43
Tibet, 32, 143
Tibullus, 128
Tigrinya language, 50, 66
time, concept of, 113
Tocqueville, Alexis
 de, 35, 38
Tolkien, J. R. R., 152
Tolstoy, Leo, 24, 38, 112
Tournier, Michael, 152
transgenderism, 9, 18, 42,
 80, 142
Trump, Donald J., 15
Turkish language, 92
Twilight books, 8

Ukrainian language, 11,
 92, 116
undergraduate curricula, 1,
 3, 5, 12, 31, 32, 47, 65, 69,

70, 77, 89, 111, 116, 136,
 145, 147, 148
urban studies, 141
Urdu language, 92

vampires, 42, 44
Vesalius, Andreas, 72
Vico, Giambattista, 38
videogames, 13–14, 121,
 126, 133
Vikings, 22
violence, political, 22,
 82, 105
Virgil, 38, 94
virtual reality, 62

Wang, Weike, 91
Warhol, Andy, 138
Washington, George, 150
Weber, Max, 35
Weimar Republic, 59, 98
West, American, 56, 94
Western Civilization, 2, 4,
 10, 22, 58, 126
Western Sahara, 32
wetlands, 81, 87
Wheatley, Phillis, 15
"white space", 32, 44
white supremacy, 75, 81, 98
whiteness, 8, 14, 23, 150
witchcraft, 20, 80, 87, 97
Wordsworth, William, 38
wrestling, 106
writing requirements, 2,
 42, 43, 111–16, 132, 133,